# *THE BLACK WATCHMAN*
# *SLEEPETH*

## by Jan Granger

EA Books Publishing

A division of Living Parables of Central Florida, Inc.

eabooksonline.com

# Table of Contents

First and foremost I give praise, thanks and honor "The Triune God" My Superhero

I would like to pay tribute to my daughter "Jazzy" who crossed life's finishing line with all of her strength, endurance and God's grace. She fought the good fight of faith, finished her race and left a legacy behind that continues to challenge and inspire those who loved her. "My soul looks back and wonder, "How she got over".

To my family, whom I love.

I give honor to Apostle F. Robinson, who encouraged me to write the vision and run with it. I give honor and thanks to Rev V. Amos who helped me "get back up again", and fine-tuned the vision. By their example, I am learning what it means to be a soldier in the army of the Lord. '

"Write down the revelation and make it plain on tablets so that a herald may run with it. For the revelation awaits an appointed time....Habakkuk 2:2b"

# The Broken Hopes of Social Activism

*"But if the watchman sees the sword coming and does not blow the trumpet to warn the people and the sword comes and takes someone's life, that person's life will be taken because of their sin, but I will hold the watchman accountable for their blood"*
(Ezekiel 33:6 NIV).

*"And do this understanding the present time: The hour has come for you to wake up from your slumber, because our salvation is nearer now than when we first believed"*
(Romans 13:11 NIV).

Every black movement that ever existed in this country, from integrationism to the various mixtures of nationalism, has failed to yield the enduring fruits for which it was intended. The solutions to our problems as a race have, for the most part, been relegated to the political, socio-economic arenas. One of the exceptions was the Civil Rights Movement, a non-violent freedom movement, which began in the South. The movement emerged out of the black church, but subsequently shifted its focus and momentum with the inclusion of other groups. Had the Civil Rights Movement maintained its focus and continued seeking God in corporate

1

sustained intercession, the history of black people would have been different.

"The Civil Rights Movement was bound for failure with all its sacrificial good works," Harold Cruse said in *Crisis of the Negro Intellectual.* "Thus, it was absolutely predictable that the Negro movement would encounter innumerable barriers, blocks and dead-ends and finally the grand impasse. One cannot have a movement in America rooted in the protest tradition, but also rife with integrationisim, separatism, interracialism, nationalism, Marxist and anti-Marxist radicalism, Communist and anti-Communist radicalism, liberalism, (Jewish and Christian) anarchism, nihilism, and religionism (the Muslim gambit) and expect such a movement not to be a failure."[1]

Conflicting and clashing theories led to the collapse of the Northern-based Civil Rights Movement, according to Cruse. So the question asked in Amos 3:3 remains relevant concerning the Civil Rights Movement: "Can two people walk together without agreeing on the direction?" (NLT). Likewise, "Jesus knew their thoughts and said to them: Any kingdom divided against itself will be ruined, and a house divided against itself will fall''. (Luke 11:17 NIV).

Since the collapse of the Civil Rights Movement, there has been no corporate voice, only a spiritual vacuum. "In the midst of all this brokenness, people are searching for answers. If we, as

---

[1] Harold Cruse, *Broken Hopes of Social Activism: Crisis of the Negro Intellectual,* (New York, William Morrow & Company, Inc., 1967), p. 403-404.

believers, do not fill the vacuum with the power and glory and the presence of God, then the vacuum will be filled with something else," Mahesh and Bonnie Chavada said in *The Watch of the Lord.*[2]

Why has it been that for the last two decades the church has engaged in bewildering silence, offering no fresh vision? Have we forgotten that, "Where there is no vision, the people perish?" (Proverbs 29:18a KJV). Social ills and moral depravity are cutting deep with lightning speed into the very heart and soul of our race. America's urban landscapes have become a fertile spawning ground—yielding a harvest of poverty, hopelessness, violence and despair. Despite the political party in office, gains that were made during the Civil Rights movement have been turned back.

The unequal distribution of wealth continues to widen in the post-civil rights era. There is unequal justice as well as income inequality with low wages and part-time jobs offering no benefits. There has been a systematic effort to dismantle public school systems in the poorest urban areas with the media heralding "doomsday budgets." In one of the poorest large cities in America, four thousand employees were laid off, which included teachers, school counselors and other personnel. A caption in a major newspaper read: "Welcome to Ground Zero. Will the Cradle of Liberty Be the Graveyard of Public Education?"

Federal cutbacks to state and city social service agencies including the private sector impact the most helpless in our society.

---

[2]Mahesh and Bonnie Chavada *The Watch of the Lord: The Secret Weapon of the Last-Day Church* (Lake Mary: Charisma House 1999), p. 63.

These services include mental healthcare, disabilities, violence protection, housing, and childcare services. These services were intended to provide a safety net for the poor. World Hunger Education Services released an article, "Hunger in America: 2015 United States Hunger and Poverty Facts," stating: "Six years after the onset of the financial and economic crisis, hunger remains high in the United States. The financial and economic crisis that erupted in 2008 caused a significant increase in hunger in the United States." This high level of hunger diminished somewhat in 2013, according to the latest government report (with the most recent statistics) released in September 2014.[3] Children were food insecure at times during the year in 9.9 percent of households with children. These 3.8 million households were unable at times during the year to provide adequate, nutritious food for their children. While children are usually shielded by their parents, who go hungry themselves, from the disrupted eating patterns and reduced food intake that characterize very low food security. Both children and adults experienced instances of very low food security in 0.9 percent of households with children "(360,000 households) in 2013.[4]

Budget cutbacks and policy changes are just a few of the factors that are contributing to the trend of rising poverty rates and inequality in America. Globalization and technology that replaces

---

[3]Coleman-Jensen, *Hunger in America: 2015 United States Hunger and Poverty Facts,* p. 1.
[4] Ibid p.2.

jobs, the decline of unions, underemployment and unemployment are also contributing factors.

Working people and the poor have experienced declines in income, while their taxes are increasing. Unions, which have historically championed the cause of the working classes, have had to struggle with those who would seek to diminish their impact.

Additionally, there are proposed cuts on the horizon. "House Bill Makes New Round of Damaging Cuts in Labor, Health and Human Services, and Education," written by David Reich and Brandon Depot for the Center on Budget and Policy Priorities states the following: "The 2016 Labor, Health and Human Services (HHS), and Education appropriations bill approved by the House Appropriations Committee provides $3.7 billion less than the year before, with the largest cuts coming in education and health. The bill eliminates or deeply cuts several major programs that aid local schools, ends grants for expanding preschool programs … In several areas the cumulative cut is even larger: K-12 education and job training, for example, are each about one-fifth below 2010 levels." Will buffers or safety nets remain for the poor? Is there a party that one can invest their hope in, that will work in the best interest of the disenfranchised, those that are marginalized. What has happened to the American dream for the middle class and blue-collar workers?

The statistics on the homeless who utilize alcohol, drug abuse, or mental illness services is 66 percent, according to the Homeless Poverty Statistics. The number of children in the U.S who live below the poverty level is 12,000,000. According to a United States Census Bureau, the official poverty measure, in 2013, 45.3 million people lived in poverty in America. This number is up from 37.3 million in 2007. This is the largest number of people living in poverty in the 52 years that these statistics have been published. Hunger continues to remain at high levels, through slightly decreased, six years after the financial and economic crisis in 2008. All the while, the face of the homeless is changing and becoming much more youthful.

A state of emergency was declared on homelessness in Los Angeles. The Los Angeles Times published an article written (2015) by Peter Jamison and David Zahniser. Seven city council members along with the mayor, Eric Garcelli, made an announcement, which was a powerful sign of the growing alarm at city hall over L.A's homeless population. It had risen 12% since 2013. "It's time to get real, because this is literally a matter of life and death," said Councilman Mike Bonin, whose westside district is home to many makeshift sidewalk encampments that are an increasingly glaring symbol of the problem across the city. He spoke of a collective failure of every level of the government to deal with what has been a homeless crisis for generations and is exploding and exacerbating now. There are estimated to be about 26,000 homeless people in L.A. The councilman continued to say, "We need to act like it's an emergency; we can't do business as usual." The number of encampments and vehicles occupied by the homeless increased to 85% over two years, according to the Los Angeles Homeless Service Authority.

There was a tech bubble, a housing bubble and now a pending student-loan crisis, all rooted in corporate greed. The Wall Street Occupy Movement sought to bring attention to the injustice of the concentration of wealth in the hands of a few, while the masses go without. More predictions of financial turbulence loom on the horizon. Hopes for the government to produce substantive change for the poor are an illusion. Politicians have set the tone for moral and ethical bankruptcy. Corporate greed has exceeded the stratosphere. Exploitation and profiting from the poor continues. The country is becoming increasingly more polarized. The poor are indeed getting poorer and the rich, richer. Where can the poor go for political redress? A more relevant question is where can the poor go for spiritual redress? Like never before, the black church should heed the calling of God born out of a sense responsibility to both God and man. This responsibility should be accompanied by a sense of urgency, for the reckoning of God for the rich and the poor is close at hand.

African Americans, like every other race, have trampled upon the mercies and grace of God. Urban cities are plagued with violent black on black crime, drug abuse, teenage pregnancy, and the breakdown of the traditional family. It has been stated that the breakdown of the family unit leads to the breakdown of society.

"Remember the law of my servant Moses, to whom at Horeb gave rules and regulations for all Israel to obey. Look, I will send you Elijah the prophet before the great and terrible day of the Lord arrives. He will encourage fathers and their children to return to me, so that I will not come and strike the earth with judgment" (Malachi 4:5-6 NET)

How can the curse of God be averted? Can it be?

# A Church Culture of Fatherlessness

*"I will get up and go to my father and say to him, "Father, I have sinned against heaven and against you ... So he got up and went to his father. But while he was still a long way from home his father saw him, and his heart went out to him; he ran and hugged his son and kissed him."*
(Luke15:18, 20 NET)

*"I have chosen him so that he may command his children and his household after him to keep the way of the Lord by doing what is right and just. Then the Lord will give to Abraham what he promised him."*
(Gen. 18:19 NET)

The spiritual imperative for the watchman in this generation is returning the hearts of the fathers to their children, and the hearts of the children to the fathers. "Fatherlessness is the most harmful demographic trend of this generation," writes David Blankenhorn in his book *Fatherless America: Confronting Our Most Urgent Social Problem.* His book is not just a criticism of fatherlessness, but of an entire culture of fatherlessness. "For in addition to losing fathers, we are losing something larger: our idea of fatherhood.

Unlike earlier periods of father absence in our history, we now face more than a physical loss affecting every home. For this reason, the most important absence our society must confront is not the absence of fathers, but the absence of our belief in fathers."[5]

I contend that the repercussions have not just a societal impact, but also a spiritual impact, reflected in the current state of the black church. The church is no stronger than the families that make up the church. Fatherlessness has a societal impact, which social agencies try to mitigate. Fathers provide spiritual coverings and protection. Fathers are given the authority from God to govern. There are spiritual roots that bind together seemingly disparate issues. Fatherlessness as an issue for African Americans finds its roots in slavery. It's easy, and preferred to forget about our past and believe there is no current connection. It pays to remember George Santayana's famous quote: "Those who cannot remember the past are condemned to repeat it"[6]

Often there are parallels in the natural and spiritual worlds. At times, Blankenhorn speaks as a cultural prophet, "In a larger sense, the fatherhood story is the irreplaceable basis of cultures most urgent imperative, the socialization of black males."[7] That is true on a natural level and a spiritual level. The Fatherhood of God story is the most urgent spiritual imperative. To fully understand

---

[5] David Blakenhorn, *Fatherless America: Confronting Our Most Urgent Social Problem* (New York: Harper Perennial, 1996), p. 1.
[6] George Santayana *The Life Of Reason,* (Prometheus Books 1905).
[7] David Blakenhorn, *Fatherless America: Confronting Our Most Urgent Social Problem* (New York: Harper Perennial, 1996), p. 1.

the fatherhood story, one must become aquatinted with the Fatherhood of God story.

In his book, Blankenhorn, lists ways the investment of fathers enriches children's lives. Fathers provide physical protection, material resources, identity, building character, daily nurturing, feeding, etc. The void and consequences produced in the absence of a father is staggering in its scope, not just within the family, but also within society at large. He goes on to state, "Concern about fatherlessness is a recurring theme in American history. As an immigrant, frontier, and slave-owning society, the United States in the eighteenth and nineteenth centuries presented harsh challenges to family life. Many children lost their parents during the journey to America. Many African American children experienced an unspeakably cruel form of father loss; forcibly separated from their fathers on the auction block."[8] Then war separated children from their fathers. In the twentieth century, the issues, he describes as a rise in "volitional fatherlessness," which is based on parental choice. He contends that America developed a culture of fatherlessness. However, I contend that issues for African American's still find their roots in the slavery experience today.

Gordon Dalbey, in his book *Healing the Masculine Soul*,[9] states the following: "In any case, the biblical faith understands that healing between fathers and children is not simply a psychological exercise to bring greater peace of mind, instead it is

[8] Ibid. p. 50.
[9] Gordon Dalbey, *Healing the Masculine Soul* (Nashville: Thomas Nelson, 1991) p. 13, 146.

the essential prerequisite to fulfill God's purposes on earth. When fathers are reconciled with sons and daughters, God's saving power is released among us; conversely when fathers and children remain at odds with one another, powers of destruction are beckoned."

So what are the powers of destruction unleashed upon the family, and if destruction is unleashed upon the family, does it not affect the church, since the church is made up of families? The issues of fatherlessness, pain, unforgiveness, bitterness, insecurity, rejection, fear abandonment, self-hatred, self-rejection, and low self-esteem all have spiritual roots manifesting in behaviors. Juvenile delinquency, pre-marital sex, teenage pregnancy depression and substance abuse find their roots in fatherlessness. It is part of the "destruction, beckoned." It manifests, spiritually, physically, emotionally and psychologically in the lives of fatherless children.

"The thief comes only to steal, kill and destroy" (John 10:10 NET).The Book of Samuel describes a type of destruction unleashed upon not only a family but on the nation as well. The prophet Eli's sons were wicked men without regard for the Lord. Furthermore, they were priests who abused their positions of authority and practiced sexual immorality. "The sin of these young men was very great in the Lord's sight, for they treated the Lord's offering with contempt" (1 Sam 2:17 NET).

Verses 22-25 of the same chapter continues: "Now Eli was very old when he heard about everything that his sons used to do to all the people of Israel and how they used to have sex with the women who were stationed at the entrance to the tent of meeting. He said to them, "Why do you behave in this way? For I hear about these evil things from all these people. This ought not to be, my sons! For the report that I hear circulating among the Lord's people is not good. If a man sins against a man, one may appeal to God on his behalf. But if a man sins against the Lord, who then will intercede for him?" But Eli's sons would not listen to their father, for the Lord had decided to kill them" (1 Sam. 2:22-25 NET).

There were consequences of destruction for the High Priest's failure to discipline his sons. Eli also failed to remove his sons from the priesthood. As a prophet, Eli knew the word of the Lord was clear: "But the person who acts defiantly, whether native-born or a resident foreigner, insults the Lord. That person must be cut off from among his people. Because he has despised the word of the Lord and has broken his commandment, that person must be completely cut off. His iniquity will be on him" (Numbers 15:30-31 NET).

Eli's sons, who sinned openly and shamelessly, should have been removed. Who knows if removing them from the office may have saved their lives and maybe they would have repented? Because of Eli's failure to father effectively, judgment came upon his home and his country.

"A man of God came to Eli and said to him, "This is what the Lord says: 'Did I not plainly reveal myself to your ancestor's house when they were in Egypt in the house of Pharaoh? I chose your ancestor from all the tribes of Israel to be my priest, to offer sacrifice on my altar, to burn incense, and to bear the ephod before me. I gave to your ancestor's house all the fire offerings made by the Israelites. Why are you scorning my sacrifice and my offering that I commanded for my dwelling place? You have honored your sons more than you have me by having made yourselves fat from the best parts of all the offerings of my people Israel'" (1 Sam. 2:27-29 NET).

Eli failed in his responsibility to provide spiritual leadership for his family. But his failure to lead his family and exercise his spiritual authority impacted his ministry and his leadership over Israel. Eli did not teach his sons to do the right thing. Failure as a father and subsequently as a minister resulted in the judgment of God against his family and Israel.

Verses 30-35 elaborates: "Therefore the Lord, the God of Israel, says, 'I really did say that your house and your ancestor's house would serve me forever.' But now the Lord says, 'May it never be! For I will honor those who honor me, but those who despise me will be cursed! In fact, days are coming when I will remove your strength and the strength of your father's house. There will not be an old man in your house! You will see trouble in my dwelling place! Israel will experience blessings, but there will not be an old man in your house for all time. Any one of you that I do not cut off from my altar, I will cause your eyes to fail and will cause you grief. All of those born to your family will die in the prime of life. This will be a confirming sign for you that will be fulfilled through your two sons, Hophni and Phinehas, in a single day they both will die! Then I will raise up for myself a faithful priest. He will do what is in my heart and soul. I will build for him a secure dynasty and he will serve my chosen one for all time" (1 Sam. 2:30-35 NET).

Samuel describes the defeat of the Israelites. The Israelites attempted to secure the Ark of the Covenant because it was known to represent the Presence of God, and therefore, was associated with victories. Israel was defeated by the Philistines and suffered heavy losses. So, the people sent for the Ark. Hophini and Phineas, Eli's sons had been wicked priests and failed to restrain the army from careless handling of the Ark. The results were that the Philistines captured the Ark in battle, and the Israelites were defeated.

"On that day a Benjaminite ran from the battle lines and came to Shiloh. His clothes were torn and dirt was on his head. When he arrived in Shiloh, Eli was sitting in his chair watching by the side of the road, for he was very worried about the ark of God. As the messenger entered the city to give his report, the whole city cried out" (1 Sam 4:12-13 NET).

Verses 14-18 continue: "When Eli heard the outcry, he said, "What is this commotion?" The man quickly came and told Eli. Now Eli was ninety-eight years old and his eyes looked straight ahead; he was unable to see. The man said to Eli, "I am the one who came from the battle lines! Just today I fled from the battle lines!" Eli asked, "How did things go, my son?" The messenger replied, "Israel has fled from the Philistines! The army has suffered a great defeat! Your two sons, Hophni and Phineas, are dead! The ark of God has been captured!" (1 Sam. 4:14-18 NET).

When Eli heard news the Ark of God had been captured, he fell backward off his chair by the city gate and died of a broken neck.

This scene is rich with symbolism.

The Bible tells us Eli 'looked straight ahead; he was unable to see.' Eli's physical and spiritual vision had become impaired. It is interesting to note that the Bible says he "fell backward" off of his chair by the gate. Eli was no longer moving forward. His neck was broken and he died. Biblical imagery associates the neck with beauty, or prosperity, authority and status. Conversely, when death is associated with the neck, as it was with Eli, it represents the loss of headship or authority. The prophet represented "headship," which means "authority and power." That day he was positioned near the gate, a place of position and authority. Eli, however, had failed to reign in his two sons, with whom he had been indulgent. They were described as wicked. When Eli heard the conclusion of the matter, he fell from his chair to the ground. It was a fall from authority. It was the failure of a father in his relationship with his sons that brought about the ruin of the Israelites, his two son's death, his own death, the wife of Phineas, and the glory of the Lord departing. The "headship, the Ark the father's, and the spiritual authority were gone. The wife of Phineas went into pre-mature labor. Was that a metaphorical representation of a woman abandoned by her husband and cast into an early labor?

The story continues in verses 19-22: "His daughter-in-law, the wife of Phineas, was pregnant and close to giving birth. When she heard that the ark of God was captured and that her father-in-law and her husband were dead, she doubled over and gave birth. But her labor pains were too much for her. As she was dying, the women who were there with her said, 'Don't be afraid! You have given birth to a son!' But she did not reply or pay any attention. She named the boy Ichabod, saying, 'The glory has departed from Israel,' referring to the capture of the ark of God and the deaths of her father-in-law and her husband. She said, 'The glory has departed from Israel, because the ark of God has been captured'" (NET).

Thus, Eli's failure to provide spiritual leadership for his family and his country adversely impacted his ministry and his leadership over Israel. His utter failure as a father and spiritual advisor ultimately resulted in God's judgment against his family and Israel.

Today, is the failure of fathers, a judgment on our race, even our nation? Will we take heed?

# Raising a Family
## Father's Role as Priest, Prophet, and King

*"But I want you to know that Christ is the head of every man, and the man is the head of a woman, and God is the head of Christ"*
(1Corinthians 11:3 NET).

*The Apostle Paul addressed the issue of this relationship in which the father is God's representative or agent on earth when he wrote about a bond or union between God and the home. The father is to represent Christ to his family. As Christ is in authority over man, the father is in authority over his family. In Christ's authoritative position as head over man, He fulfilled three major ministries: priest, prophet and king. Paul also admonishes us to "Be imitators of me, just as I also am of Christ"*
(1Corinthians 11:1 NET).

Dr. Derek Prince, a spiritual father too many and an international Bible teacher, contributed significantly to the topic of both spiritual and natural fatherhood. He describes the role of fathers as the one who represents God to his family and who represents his family to God. Like Paul, Prince also examines the father's role in the family as that of priest, prophet and king. It is the priestly duty of the father to represent his family before God. The father, in his role as prophet, represents God to his family. As king, he rules his family on behalf of God.[10]

## Fathers Function as Priest
## "It's a Family Affair, It's A Family Affair"
Sly and the Family Stone

*"To Him who loves us and has freed us from our sins by His blood, and has made us to be a kingdom and priests to serve His God and Father-to Him be glory and power forever and ever! Amen"*
(Rev. 1:6 NIV).

*"Let the priests, those who serve the Lord, weep from the vestibule all the way back to the altar. Let them say, "Have pity, O Lord, on your people; please do not turn over your inheritance to be mocked"*
(Joel 2:17b NET).

Exodus 40 outlines a model of the Priesthood of the Tabernacle. "'Then you are to clothe Aaron with the holy garments and anoint him and sanctify him so that he may minister as my priest. You are to bring his sons and clothe them with tunics and anoint them just as you anointed their father, so that they may minister as my priests; their anointing will make them a priesthood

---

[10] Derek Prince, "Knowing God as Father" (Derek Prince Ministries International, 1981)

that will continue throughout their generations.' This is what Moses did, according to all the Lord had commanded him – so he did" (Exodus 40:13-16 NET).

In the heavenly tabernacle, Christ is our High Priest, while also serving as the Perfect Sacrifice. The writer of Hebrews clearly states as such: "But now Christ has come as the high priest of the good things to come. He passed through the greater and more perfect tent not made with hands, that is, not of this creation, and he entered once for all into the most holy place not by the blood of goats and calves but by his own blood, and so he himself secured eternal redemption. For if the blood of goats and bulls and the ashes of a young cow sprinkled on those who are defiled consecrated them and provided ritual purity, how much more will the blood of Christ, who through the eternal Spirit offered himself without blemish to God, purify our consciences from dead works to worship the living God" (Hebrews 9:11-14 NET). The priesthood was made up of Aaron, consecrated with oil to be the High Priest and his sons. It is important to note that the priesthood was a hereditary office. God is all about the family. High Priest wore a breastplate, the ephod bedecked with twelve stones, representing the twelve tribes, and a turban with an inscription graved unto a gold plate. The words engraved on it read, "HOLINESS TO THE LORD." The Priesthood was a family affair.

The Book of Samuel gives us an account of King David's failure to know how to handle the sacred Presence of God. May we all learn from his mistake. The narrative unfolds concerning the Ark: "When they arrived at the threshing floor of Nacon, Uzzah reached out and grabbed hold of the ark of God, because the oxen stumbled. 6:7 The Lord was so furious with Uzzah, he killed him on the spot for his negligence. He died right there beside the ark of God. David was angry because the Lord attacked Uzzah; so he called that place Perez Uzzah, which remains its name to this very day. David was afraid of the Lord that day and said, 'How will the ark of the Lord ever come to me?' So David was no longer willing to bring the ark of the Lord to be with him in the City of David. David left it in the house of Obed-Edom the Gittite" (2 Sam. 6:6-10 NET). David knew how to function as King, but King David had to learn to function as a Priest. How many losses have we suffered due to a "lack of knowledge?"

Hosea issues an admonishment from God: "My people are destroyed from lack of knowledge. 'Because you have rejected knowledge, I also reject you as my priests; because you have ignored the law of your God, I also will ignore your children'" (Hosea 4:6 NIV). Notice the connection between the failure of the priest and the effect on the children. The chief obligation of the father as priest is to offer sacrifices for his family. The model of priests and the offering of sacrifices are found in the Old Testament. One such example is found in the life of Job. Job is described as a blameless and upright man, who feared God and shunned evil. He had seven sons and three daughters. Job's sons took turns holding feasts and fellowships in their homes, inviting their sisters.

"Now his sons used to go and hold a feast in the house of each one in turn, and they would send and invite their three sisters to eat and to drink with them. When the days of their feasting were finished, Job would send for them and sanctify them; he would get up early in the morning and offer burnt offerings according to the number of them all. For Job thought, 'Perhaps my children have sinned and cursed God in their hearts.' This was Job's customary practice" (Job 1:4-5 NET). Herein is a model of a father fulfilling his duty to intercede for his family, as every father should. We could easily see a mother doing that, but what about dad?

In The Book of Exodus, we find God's provision of the Passover. The significance of Passover is that the Lord would not destroy those living in houses that were under the sign of blood. They would be delivered through the provision a sacrificial Passover Lamb. Israel would be delivered from the agent of judgment, a destroying angel upon Egyptian gods. The judgment came upon every Egyptian home and struck down their first-born. The passage in Exodus 12:3 states "speak ye unto all the congregation of Israel saying, 'In the tenth day of this month they shall take to them every man a lamb, according to the house.'" The father as the head of the household, was responsible for selecting and slaying the Lamb. He also had the responsibility for sprinkling its blood with hyssop on the top and sides of the doorframe. Thus the father had the role of the priest on behalf of his family. By sprinkling the blood on the doorpost, he was ensuring the safety and protection of his family.

Where there is no father or male representative, the family goes unprotected. In light of our present day culture that means scores of black youth are without a spiritual and physical covering. Black boys adapt to a subculture of violence and hardness to protect themselves physically and emotionally. You can't blame the children who are engaging survival techniques. This role of priest cannot be delegated to another person in the family. The federal government can't do it, or the social service agents. Neither psychiatrist, nor therapist can replace the father. When fathers are gone, it's everybody loss.

## Vision of the High Priest

This was a vision that was related to Joshua, who was a High Priest in his time who represented the nation of Israel to God. "Then he showed me Joshua the high priest standing before the angel of the Lord, and Satan standing at his right side to accuse him. The Lord said to Satan "The Lord rebuke you, Satan! The Lord who has chosen Jerusalem, rebuke you! Is not this man a burning stick snatched from the fire" (Zechariah 3:2 NIV)? Now Joshua was dressed in fifty clothes as he stood before the angel.

The angel said to those who were standing before him, take off his fifty clothes." Then he said to Joshua, "See, I have taken away your sin, and I will put rich garments on you." Then I said, "Put a clean turban on his head." So they put a clean turban on his head and clothed him, while the angel of the Lord stood by.

The opposition to the high priest is represented here by Satan. Himself. The priest in his own strength cannot withstand the opposer. Note that the priest is dressed with fifty clothes which is symbolic of "sin". Israel became a burning stick that God snatched from the fires of sufferings and judgement. God removed the fifty clothing of the priest, dressed him with clean clothes and restored the role as a high priest. Thus the high priest is once again able to fulfill his role as an intercessor and restorer of the relationship between God and His people. So, it can be for the father that seeks to function in his role as priest for his family.

**Fathers Function as Prophet**

*"For who has stood in the counsel of the Lord, And perceived and heard His word? Who has marked His word and heard it?"*
(Jeremiah 23: 18 CLB).

*"But if they had stood in My counsel, And had caused My people to hear My Words, Then they would have turned from their evil way And from the evil of their doings. Am I a God near at hand," says*

*the Lord "And not a God afar off? So I shall not see him?" says the Lord. "Do I not fill heaven and earth?" says the Lord"* (Jeremiah 23:22-24 CLB).

*"Yet which of them has ever stood in the Lord's inner circle so they could see and hear what he has to say? Which of them have ever paid attention or listened to what he has said?"* (Jeremiah 23:18 NET).

*"But if they had stood in my inner circle, they would have proclaimed my message to my people. They would have caused my people to turn from their wicked ways and stop doing the evil things they are doing. 'Do you think that I am some local deity and not the transcendent God?' the Lord asks. 'Do you really think anyone can hide himself where I cannot see him?' the Lord asks. 'Do you no know that I am everywhere?' the Lord asks"* (Jeremiah 23:22-24 NET).

As the father functions as prophet, his responsibility is as God's representative to his family. Whether good or bad, that's what a father does by default. Our impressions of God extend from our impressions of our earthly father. If dad is aloof and indifferent, that's pretty much how we view God. If our father is loving, tender and affirming, that's also how we view God. So a father can misrepresent what the true nature of God is like. What must we do concerning our "misrepresentation of God? Repent and turn around. Fathers need to assume their roles as God's representative in the family again.

**Fathers Function as King**

*"For the King trusts in the Lord; through the unfailing love of the Most High, he will not be shaken"*
(Psalms 21:7 NIV).

*"The father's function as king is one who governs his family with God's interest at heart. The father directs, decides, guides, and influences from a position of God-given authority. The Apostle Paul tells us a father "must manage his own family well and see that his children obey him with proper respect"* (1 Tim 3:4 NIV)

If a man can't manage his family he does not qualify to be a church elder. There is the saying that a church is no stronger than the families in it. Abraham is a wonderful example of someone who governed his family well, and as a result, became head of a nation.

"Then the Lord said, 'Should I hide from Abraham what I am about to do? After all, Abraham will surely become a great and powerful nation, and all the nations on the earth will pronounce blessings on one another using his name. I have chosen him so that he may command his children and his household after him to keep the way of the Lord by doing what is right and just. Then the Lord will give to Abraham what he promised him'" (Genesis 18:17-19 NET). Abraham's original name was Abram, meaning "exalted father" Abraham could be trusted by God to be father to his family and to nations.

Fathers need to rise up and assume all three roles God has given them—priest, prophet and king—for their children.

## Returning the Children's Hearts to the Father

Significantly, it is the fathers and not the mothers upon whom God focuses His call for reconciliation in the last days."[11] It is the bonding of the father and the children that is the spiritual imperative. It is the father that is responsible and should provide direction for the family. Ted Dobson in his article "Healing the Tear in the Masculine Soul,"[12] traces "the brokenness in men to the fact that boys lack sufficient contact with their fathers to generate a healthy self-image. Thus, he concludes that the "tear"–a gaping hole or wound—leads to profound insecurity. The German psychologist, Alexander Mitscherlich, has written that society has torn the soul of the male, and into this tear demons have fled—demons of insecurity, selfishness, and despair. Consequently, men

---

[11]David Blakenhorn, *Fatherless America: Confronting Our Most Urgent Social Problem* (New York: Harper Perennial, 1996) p. 146.
[12] Ted Dobson "Healing the Tear in the Masculine Soul," (SCRC Vision, April 1985).

do not know who they are as men." While Dalbey and Dobson address the natural relationship between fathers and children, it is more imperative in the spiritual realm. The black church must reconcile with the "Fatherhood of God," restoring faith in the Heavenly Father, who desires an intimate relationship with us. In the Book of Job, it is stated "Oh, for the days when I was in my prime, when God's intimate friendship blessed my house" (Job 29:4 NIV).

I can attest that growing up fatherless affected my entire family. My mother kept a roof over our head, but there were many times when there was a food shortage. I remember sitting in a cold, scantly furnished apartment while my mother was working and eating the starch that she used for ironing her uniforms. I resorted to eating starch when we ran out of sugar or mustard sandwiches, which we often made. My mother took out a loan to purchase graduation clothes for my siblings and I. A graduation she couldn't attend because she had to be at work. My sister would talk of suicide, not understanding the source of her pain. I struggled in school lacking motivation. My mother was too worn out from working so hard to help me with schoolwork. My brother was bullied into joining a gang that provided companionship, but which also lead him down the wrong path. We had no gatekeeper, no protector, no spiritual or natural covering.

In Deuteronomy, we see a picture of the close relationship God desires "Let the beloved of the Lord rest secure in Him, for He shields him all day long and the one the Lord loves rest between His shoulders" (Deut. 33:12 NIV). Our security is in resting between His shoulders." At the Lord's Supper, we see John, a disciple, reclining on Jesus's shoulders. Peter turned around and saw the disciple whom Jesus loved following them. (This was the disciple who had leaned back against Jesus' chest at the meal and asked, "Lord, who is the one who is going to betray you?)" (John 21:20 NET).

It's not that the other disciples did not love Jesus, but John pressed into a more intimate relationship with him. He is referred to as "the Beloved." It is that relationship that sustained John, such that he remained close by even during the crucifixion. "When Jesus saw His mother there, and the disciple whom He loved, standing nearby, He said to His mother, 'Woman, look, here is your son,' and to the disciple 'Look, here is your mother'" (John 19:26-27 NET). This is the type of relationship that the Father desires of us. Those who are "the beloved of God" find safety, security, and identity as they rest between His shoulders. Psalms 91 assures us that "He that dwelled in the secret place of the Most High shall abide in the shadow of the Almighty. He will cover you with His feathers and under His wings you will find refuge." One of God's names is El Shaddai, meaning Almighty or God All Sufficient, but also translated as "breast." God is known as the Many Breasted One, which reveals the character of God as One who is all-sufficient to nourish, supply and also satisfy. The Presence of God becomes our ultimate satisfaction and safe house against the onslaught of the enemy.

I am reminded of the old gospel hymn sung by many church choirs, "Leaning on The Everlasting Arms." The lyrics capture the experience of resting upon The Many Breasted One.

> What a fellowship, what a joy divine,
>
> leaning on the everlasting arms.
>
> What blessedness, what a peace is mine,
>
> leaning on the everlasting arms.
>
> Leaning, Leaning,
>
> Safe and secure from all alarms;
>
> Leaning, leaning,
>
> Leaning on the everlasting arms.[13]

The soul of the church is in need of healing. The root cause is a lack of knowledge concerning our Father God. The Bible says, "My people are destroyed for lack of knowledge; because you have rejected knowledge, I reject you from being a priest to me. And since you have forgotten the law of your God, I also will forget your children" (Hosea 4:6 ESV). This was the charge that was brought against Israel's Prophets. It is an indictment against us as well. The cost for us as a people has been staggering. The Prophet Hosea admonished the people: "Let us acknowledge the Lord: Let us press on to acknowledge him. As surely as the sun rises, He will appear; He will come to us like the winter rains, like the spring

---

[13] *Leaning on the Everlasting Arms* is a hymn published in 1887 with music and lyrics by Anthony J. Showalter and Elisha Hoffman.

rains that water the earth" (Hosea 6:3 NIV). There must be a "press" to enter into the Presence of the Lord.

I did not grow up in my father's house, nor did most of my peers. I grew up wondering why my father did not want me. There were so few peers that had a father at home that I thought those children who did have dads must have been very privileged. Let's take a look at the "Fatherhood of God" story.

**Fatherhood: A Divine Initiative**

I want to know who love is
I want You to show me.

*"Now this is eternal life—that they know you, the only true God, and Jesus Christ, whom you sent"*
(John 17:3 NET).

*"The church knows Jesus, but does not know God as Father. The Jews know God, but don't know Jesus"*
– Rabbi Landry

*"Behold what manner of love the Father has bestowed on us, that we should be called children of God! And such we are"*
(1 John 3:1a ASV).

*"And I will be a father to you, and you will be my sons and daughters," says the All-Powerful Lord"*
(2 Corinthians 6:18 NET).

*"Even if my father and mother abandoned me, the LORD would take me in"*
(Psalm 27:10 NET).

Fatherhood is not a cultural contrivance, as suggested by Blankenhorn, but it is in fact, a divine initiative of God. Before anyone can fully grasp the human role in fatherhood, one must grasp an understanding of the "Fatherhood of God" story. According to Derek Prince, in his transcript entitled the "Fatherhood of God," the Fatherhood of God is the great fact behind the entire universe. That there exists a Father, who is our God, is the fact or actuality behind all other facts and that "Father" has left His impression on every element of the universe."

This is the actuality that motivated Paul's prayer found in Ephesians: "For this cause I bow my knees unto the Father of our Lord Jesus Christ from whom the whole family in heaven and earth derives its name" (Ephesians 3:14-15 KJV). Thus, the concept of Fatherhood is derived directly from "God the Father." God the Father has a Son named Jesus Christ and their relationship precedes time and creation. The Gospel of John says: "In the beginning was the word and the Word was with God, and the Word was God He was with God in the beginning" (John 1:1-2

NIV). We gain insight into the relationship of God the Father and His Son, Jesus. This sets the pattern for all father and son relationships. We also get a glimpse of the uniqueness of Christianity, which is characterized by a rich, close relationship that a child of God can have with a loving, yet omnipotent Father God.

This loving intimate relationship is made possible through God's Son, Jesus Christ. Jesus's purpose for entering humanity was to reveal the Father's love and make reconciliation available to all. Reconciliation and relationship was and remains the mission of Jesus. This is not to be a causal affair. Jesus invested His lifeblood into attaining the type of relationship that satisfies our deepest longings and needs: to love and be loved. In 1 Peter it states, "For Christ also died for sins, once and for all, the righteous for the unrighteous, to bring us to God" (Peter 3:18 NIV). Jesus provides the way to God and says, "I Am the way and the truth and the life. No one comes to the Father except through Me" (John 14:6 NIV). Jesus declares His purpose in coming: "I have manifested thy name to the men whom thou gavest Me out of the world" (John 17:9 NIV). "I will remain in the world no longer and I am coming to you, Holy Father. Protect them by the power of Your name—the name you gave Me—so that they may be one" (John 1:7,11 NIV). In John 1:26, Jesus says of His mission "I have made You known to them, and will continue to make You known in order that the love You have for Me may be in them, that I myself may be in them," (NIV).

What was so extraordinary concerning that name that made it distinct from all the other names of God in the Old Testament? The name revealed the nature of the relationship that God desired as "Father". According to Derek Prince the name of Father is the ultimate name of God, that describes the nature of God in His eternal character more perfectly than any other word that exists in the human language. So the Fatherhood behind all "human fatherhood's and the reality behind all families is the Fatherhood of God," according to Derek Prince.

In the absence of a father, children lose out on many things that are necessary for their development. Self-worth, protection and identity are a few of those things. "The church knows Jesus, but they do not know God as Father," has been my experience in the Pentecostal church. I was introduced to Jesus, and God as Father, but did not develop in my knowledge of God as Father. Being fatherless actually fueled my desire to have a relationship with God, but it also tainted my perception of who Father God is. I made little effort at knowing God as Father. For many years there was a disconnect, and I struggled to trust God. I wrote about my experience with fatherlessness, but didn't know how to resolve the issue. I had the opportunity to attend a "For My Life" retreat. The teaching of "The Father's Love "brought much healing to my wounded soul. The first order of ministry was to deal with the issues of fatherlessness. We were taught on the impact of fatherlessness, the love of the Father, and the need for reconciliation. Reconciliation was considered vital in rebuilding the spiritual foundation of our lives. I attended the retreat for other painful issues and had no idea that this was the root cause in so many other seemingly disparate issues, and knew that this teaching was very much needed. This model of "reconciliation to the Fatherhood of God should be repeated in most churches across the nation, but particularly in the black church. There must be an acknowledgement of the pain, disappointment, deep wounds and broken heart that that type of rejection can bring. With it comes emotional and spiritual bondage, which requires deliverance and healing of the soul. There must be a restoration of Father, son/daughter relationships. We must take back our belief in the Fatherhood of God and develop a culture of honor for the Fatherhood of God and our natural fathers. It is in that relationship where the self-worth, protection, security, and identity will be restored. It is also in that place where the vision for the church to move forward will be unfolded.

The Father said to Jesus, His Son: "This is My Son, whom I love; with Him I am well pleased" (Matthew 3:16 NIV). How many of us are yearning to hear a statement of love, identity, ownership, and affirmation? Jesus knew that His Father loved Him. We need that too.


*"Why were you looking for me? Didn't you know that I must be in my Father's house?"*
(Luke 2:49 NET).

*"Jesus answered, 'Even if I testify about myself, my testimony is true, because I know where I came from and where I am going'"*
(John 8:14a NET).

*"But as for me, because of your great faithfulness I will enter your house; I will bow down toward your holy temple as I worship you"*
(Psalm 5:7 NET).

*"You will bring them in and plant them in the mountain of your inheritance, in the place you made for your residence, O Lord, the sanctuary, O LORD, that your hands have established"*
(Exodus 15:17 NET).

*"Blessed are those who dwell in Your house"*
(Psalm 84:4a NIV).

*"A fountain will flow out of the Lord's house and will water the valley of acacias"*
(Joel 3:18 NIV).

It's time for the black church to return to our Father's house. The psalmist describes a people hungry for the presence of God, longing to be near Him and desiring to be in the Father's house. "How lovely is the place where you live, O LORD who rules over all? I desperately want to be in the courts of the LORD's temple.

My heart and my entire being shout for joy to the living God" (Psalm 84:1-2 NET).

My soul thirsts for God, for the living God. When can I go and meet with God? My soul thirsts for God. "As a deer longs for streams of water, so I long for you, O God!" (Psalm 42:2 NET). The psalmist compares the need for water to sustain life equally with the need for the presence of God to sustain us spiritually.

A son learns from his father, and in this example, Solomon learned from his father David: "Listen, children, to a father's instruction, and pay attention so that you may gain discernment. Because I give you good instruction, do not forsake my teaching. When I was a son to my father, a tender only child before my mother, he taught me, and he said to me: 'Let your heart lay hold of my words; keep my commands so that you will live'" (Proverbs 4:1-4 NET).

# The Complacency of Black Zion:
# We Do Not Grieve Over the Ruin of Joseph

*"And it came to pass, when Joseph was come unto his brethren, that they striped Joseph out of his coat, his coat of many colors that was on him; And they took him, and cast him into a pit: and the pit was empty, there was no water in it"* (Genesis 37:23-24 KJV).

*"That drink wine in bowls, and anoint themselves with the chief ointments: but they are not grieved for the affliction of Joseph"* (Amos 6:6b KJV).

*"And they said unto me, 'The remnant that are left of the captivity there in the province are in great affliction and reproach: the wall of Jerusalem also is broken down, and the gates thereof are burned with fire.' And it came to pass, when I heard these words, that I sat down and wept, and mourned certain days; and I fasted and prayed before the God of heaven"*

(Nehemiah 1:3-4 ASV).

*"Oh that my head were waters, and mine eyes a fountain of tears, that I might weep day and night for the slain of the daughter of my people!"*
(Jeremiah 9:1 ASV).

The complacency of black Zion refers to the silence of the black church. Since the Civil Rights Movement, the black church has failed to step forward as a corporate entity with a unified voice offering fresh vision during trying times. Little has changed in the last two decades. There still remains a deafening silence. The African-American man in this country has been vividly depicted as a man bearing the yoke of oppression across his shoulders. The struggles of the black man have been complex and multifaceted. Yet, we who lay claim to the "anointing of God"—which we know destroys yokes—remain silent. Our silence has been towards God and towards our race. Isaiah 59:1 states, "Look, the Lord's hand is not too weak to deliver you; his ear is not too deaf to hear you" (NET). Many black Christians, by virtue of our relationship with the Lord, have prospered and broken through the walls of poverty and despair. God has blessed us with a degree of comfort and security. Within that comfort zone we have peacefully submitted to the spiritual status quo of injustice and oppression, for ourselves and for our brothers. This attitude is manifested through our complacency, and prayerlessness in addressing our issues in a collective way. There's been no collective solemn assembly to seek God as to the spiritual roots underlying behaviors that on the surface appear to be disconnected. But first, we as a church must get to the roots of our own behaviors and why we respond in the manner in which we have or have not. In doing so we may find common ground. In the Book of Amos, God sharply rebukes his people for such attitudes:

"Woe to you who are complacent in Zion, and to you who feel secure on Mount Samaria, you notable men of the foremost nation to whom the people of Israel come. Go to Calneh and look at it: go from there to great Hamath, and then go down to Gath in Philistia. Are they better off than your two kingdoms? Is their land larger than yours? You put off the evil day and bring near a reign of terror. You lie on beds inlaid with ivory and lounge on your couches. You dine on choice lambs and fattened calves. You strum away on your harps like David and improvise on musical instruments. You drink wine by the bowlful and use your finest lotions, but you do grieve over the ruin of Joseph" (Amos 6:1-6 NIV).

As God rebuked Israel through His prophet Amos for their complacency, so God is speaking to us. Our individual and collective sin has been allowing this spiritual stupor to continue. Has this become another black on black crime? According to Derek Prince in his radio program, *Ruling by Prayer*,[14] there has to

[14] Derek Prince Legacy Radio, *Ruling by Prayer*, http://www.derekprince.org/Articles/1000133552/DPM_US/Radio_15/DPLR_1 5_Archives/Ruling_By_Prayer/Ruling_By_Prayer.aspx

be an acknowledgement of our sins of omission, our failure to do the right thing. We have not grieved over the losses, affliction, enslavement, and the ruin of our brothers—the epidemic. Yes, there is violence, fatherlessness, drug abuse and more, which are manifestations with spiritual roots. As a church we need to "Selah," to pause and think about that. What have we overlooked, or maybe the question should be, what have we looked at and ignored? Despite the fact there are so many churches in our neighborhoods, with all of our churchgoing we have remained self-centered and consumed with regressive individualistic attitudes. Increasingly little to no concern has extended beyond the boundaries of our own family and friends. Our attitudes have been "us for and no time or concern for anymore." Once again, we find a scathing indictment aimed at the people of God in Isaiah 56:10-12: " His watchmen are blind: they are all ignorant, they are all dumb dogs, they cannot bark; sleeping, lying down, loving to slumber. Yea, they are greedy dogs which can never have enough, and they are shepherds that cannot understand: they all look to their own way, every one for his gain, from his quarter. Come ye, say they, I will fetch wine, and we will fill ourselves with strong drink; and tomorrow shall be as this day, and much more abundant" (KJV). As good Christians we have not likely been consumed by wine literally. But we have been inebriated and consumed into a culture of apathy, complicacy, and indifference while our race sinks deeper into spiritual crisis. We have lacked vision, fresh revelation, discernment, and understanding. It's time to wake up, as the passage states in Isaiah.

*"Awake, awake! Put on your strength, Zion. Put on your beautiful garments, Jerusalem, the holy city: for from now on the uncircumcised and the unclean will no more come into you"*
(Isaiah 52:1 WEB).

## Call to Repentance and Humility

*"... if my people, who are called by my name, will humble themselves, pray, seek my face, and turn from their wicked ways; then I will hear from heaven, will forgive their sin, and will heal their land"*
(II Chronicles 7:14 WEB).

*"Be watchful, and strengthen the things which remain, that are ready to die: for I have not found thy works perfect before God. Remember therefore how thou hast received and heard, and hold fast, and repent. If therefore thou shalt not watch, I will come on thee as a thief, and thou shalt not know what hour I will come upon thee"*

(Revelation 3:2-3 KJV).

In Walter Wink's article entitled "History Belongs to the Intercessors" he describes prayer in short as the theater in which the "diseased spirituality" that we have contracted from the powers can best be diagnosed and treated by God who offers all of this in His word and therein lays the answer. God's diagnosis of the disease is sin, and the treatment is repentance and self-humbling. As with any treatment, success is conditional upon following the prescribed remedy. The directive of God begins with who He says qualifies to approach Him. He says "If My People," and if there is further need for clarification, He says "who are called by My Name." Unlike the blend of ideological factions that came together during the Civil Rights era, God says, "My people called by my name." The second condition is that we must humble ourselves before our God. James 4:6b, states that God resists the proud, and gives grace to the humble. We must defer to God's conditions of humility, understanding His sovereignty and our limitations, and our inability to effect substantive, enduring change for ourselves. This type of humility is expressed by Jehoshaphat as he prayed in II Chronicles 20:12: "Our God, will you not judge them? For we are powerless against this huge army that attacks us! We don't know what we should do; we look to you for help" (NET).

In II Chronicles 14:11 it says, "Asa prayed to the Lord his God: 'O Lord, there is no one but you who can help the weak when they are vastly outnumbered. Help us, O Lord our God, for we rely on you and have marched on your behalf against this huge army. O Lord our God, don't let men prevail against you!" (NET). Asa's prayer expresses where we find ourselves today as a people. We are powerless against those who would seek to exploit and profit from the losses of the poor. We dare not rely upon our strength, which is at best woefully inadequate. Our foes are formidable and relentless. For us to believe that we, through reliance on any political or social-economic system, will prevail is a deception, and in fact has never happened. In Hosea 10:13-14a, God's word states the following:

"But you have planted wickedness, you have reaped evil, you have eaten the fruit of deception. Because you have depended on your own strength and on your many warriors, the roar of battle will rise against your people, so that all your fortresses will be devastated—" (NIV).

In Jeremiah we learn that after the conditions of repentance and humility have been met then are we free to pray fervently, earnestly seeking God. Seeking God's face entails more than occasional prayer meetings. Hosea 10:12 addresses the issue of seeking God, "Sow to yourselves in righteousness, reap according to kindness. Break up your fallow ground; for it is time to seek Yahweh, until he comes and rains righteousness on you" (WEB). Here we are admonished to seek the Lord until He comes. The objective is to pray concerning these issues until we have heard from God. It is unrelenting, persistent, and hammering away in prayer. An excellent example is found in Psalm 18:37,42 where David says "I have pursued mine enemies, and overtaken them: neither did I turn again till they were consumed; Then did I beat them small as the dust before the wind: I did cast them out as the dirt in the streets" (KJV). In II Kings 13:17-20 Jehoash met with moderate victory because he lacked the persistence and fervency to accomplish the task as directed by Elisha. The scene unfolds in II Kings 13:17-20 "And he said, 'Open the window eastward.' And he opened it. Then Elisha said, 'Shoot.' And he shot. And he said, 'The arrow of the LORD's deliverance, and the arrow of deliverance from Syria: for thou shalt smite the Syrians in Aphek, till thou have consumed them.' And he said, 'Take the arrows.' And he took them. And he said unto the king of Israel, 'Smite upon the ground.' And he smote thrice, and stayed. And the man of God was wroth with him, and said, 'Thou shouldest have smitten five or six times; then hadst thou smitten Syria till thou hadst consumed it: whereas, now thou shalt smite Syria but thrice.' And Elisha died, and they buried him. And the bands of the Moabites invaded the land at the coming in of the year" (KJV). As a result of this partial victory, Jeroboam II, Jehoash"s son, was left to deal with the enemy at a later date. In a similar fashion the Civil Rights Movement had a degree of success, but it was partial, so we find ourselves dealing with the same enemies today.

# The Black Watchman Sleepeth

*"So I sought for a man among them who would that should make up the hedge, stand in the gap before me on behalf of the land so that I should not destroy it: but I found none"*

(Ezekiel 22:30 KJV).

*"If therefore thou shalt not watch, I will come on thee as a thief, and thou shalt not know the hour I will come upon thee"*

(Revelation 3:3 KJV).

*"So then, let us not like others, who are asleep, but let us be alert..."*

(1 Thessalonians 5:6 NIV).

*"But Jonah had gone down below deck, where he lay down and fell into a deep sleep. The captain went to him and said, "How can you sleep? Get up and call on your God! Maybe He will take notice of us, and we will not perish'"*

(Jonah 1:55,6 NIV).

In the Hebrew language "watching" refers to "wakefulness." It
is the practice of remaining awake while others sleep. The words
"watch," "watching," and "watchmen," occur with frequency in
the Old and New Testaments. Directives are given to the church to
"be watchful, awake, and vigilant" to what is going on concerning
the welfare of our nation, churches, and families. To "watch" is a
warlike term that refers to a sentry or guard. Watchmen are not just
to be alert, but prepared to carry out the directives of the Lord.
Watchmen have been authorized by God and are called to occupy
pivotal positions on the wall. Spiritual Watchers are called to pray
and stand in the gap for the people of God, our churches, families,
and nations. The Watchman is looking to see who is advancing
towards the city. In 2 Samuel 18:26 it states "And the watchman
saw another man running; and the watchman called unto the porter,
and said, Behold, another man running alone. And the king said,
He also bringeth tidings. 'So the watchman saw another man
running, but at a further distance. The watchman is able to see
further because of his positioning up on the wall. The watchman
must stay awake, alert, vigilant, and not allow for distraction'"
(ASV). Watching, Watchnight Prayer, or "All night prayer," as it is
often referred to in black churches, speaks to a certain type of
prayer. As a young woman I experienced this type of prayer in the
Pentecostal church I attended. The church mothers would walk the
floors all night long from midnight until six in the morning,
singing and praying in the spirit. They labored in prayer, until they
prayed through. I learned valuable life lessons in that church. In

my most difficult of times I would always return to that place of prayer, which sustained me from going under the rip currents of life. The tradition of Watchnight Prayer is a part of African American history. Even before President Lincoln issued the Emancipation Proclamation, enslaved men and women observed some form of watchnight prayer.

Freedom Songs, praying, and sermons were a part of those services. It was, and remains today, a time that suffering was and is shared horizontally and vertically. It was a time to share the faithfulness of our God. It was a time to fight the good fight of faith. It was a time for "praying through." It was and is a 'fire by night.' This is a practice that we as a people must return to if we are to not just "survive" the coming storm, but also be "more than conquerors." Black people sacrificed sleep to seek God for preparation of that which "could be." The "Watch" became a part of a survival or coping mechanism. That specific type of prayer, born out of sacrifice, strengthened them with the type of mental, spiritual, and emotional fortitude they needed to endure incredible losses and unrelenting pain. There was a synergy of unity and of purpose. They had mourned their losses but they refused to tire. Jesus said to His disciples, who were given to slumber in the Garden of Gethsemane, "Watch and pray so that you fall not into temptation. The spirit is willing, but the body is weak" (Mark 14:38 NIV). Our enslaved brothers and sisters knew that in their own strength they could not overcome the obstacles. We can only sing "We have Overcome" in truth if we follow Jesus's example.

So we must be watchful, alert, and vigilant, and we must practice that particular form of prayer." Think of a night watchman or a guard that comes on duty at night. One sacrifices his or her sleep in order to spend time in the Presence of God, interceding on behalf of others in prayer. The Bible refers to four watches, broken up into 3 hourly sections. The first is 6pm to 9pm, the second is 9pm to 12am, the third is 12am to 3am, and the last is 3am to 6am. Mark 6:48 states: "and about the fourth watch of the night he cometh unto them, walking upon the sea, and would have passed by them" (KJV). Thus, there are also nights into early morning watches. Much has been written on the contentions that occur during each particular watch of the night. According to Rick Joyner, the biblical positions of the watchman were (1) on the walls of the city (Isaiah 62:6-7) (2) walking about in the city. (Song of Solomon 3:3) and (3) on the hills or in the countryside (Jeremiah 31:6).

**The Watchman and the Gatekeepers need to both be in their positions.**

*"All these which were chosen to be porters in the gates were two hundred and twelve. These were reckoned by their genealogy in*

*their villages, whom David and Samuel the seer did ordain in their*
*set office"*
(1Chronicles 9:22 KJV).

*"For the Son of Man is as a man taking a far journey, who left his*
*house, and gave authority to his servants, and to every man his*
*work, and commanded the porter to watch"* (Mark 13:34 KJV).

*"For a day in your courts is better than a thousand.*
*I would rather be a doorkeeper in the house of my God,*
*than to dwell in the tents of wickedness"*
(Psalm 84:10 WEB).

*"Lift up your heads, you gates! Be lifted up, you everlasting doors,*
*and the King of glory will come in"*
(Psalm 24:7 WEB).

Gatekeepers in the Old Testament were spoken about in relationship to the Temple of God. They were assigned to the Temple. Their duty was to guard the entrances, being responsible for all four directions: the east, west, north, and south. This was described as a "trusted office" and there were four chief gatekeepers, who were all Levites. They lived in the chambers around the house of God to guard the temple, and they had to open up every morning. There is so much symbolism, which speaks to the close relationship they had with the Presence of God. They had various duties, which included charge over the serving vessels, furnishings, the sanctuary, and the fine flour for preparing showbread for every Sabbath. Then there were singers—heads of the father's houses of the Levites, who lodged in the chambers. These singers were employed day and night. In I Chronicles 23:5 it states: "Four-thousand are to be gatekeepers; and 4,000 are to praise the Lord with the instruments I supplied for worship" (NET). This was David's instruction to his son, Solomon, in the building of the Temple. The gatekeepers as well as watchman are types of prophetic intercessors. We see in the life of Habakkuk as he stated:

"I will stand upon my watch, and set me upon the tower, and will look forth to see what he will speak with me, and what I shall answer concerning my complaint. And Jehovah answered me, and said, "Write the vision, and make it plain upon tablets, that he may run that readeth it. For the vision is yet for the appointed time, and it hasteth toward the end, and shall not lie: though it tarry, wait for it; because it will surely come, it will not delay" (2: 1-3 ASV).

Failing to "keep watch" as a gatekeeper or watchmen had consequences, which are evident in the Old and New Testaments. God's message is to the church in I Thessalonians 5:6: "Therefore let us not sleep, as do others; but let us watch and be sober" (KJV). The assignment given to the church is to watch and pray. The authority has already been delegated to the church, Christ's body. Jesus stated, "On this rock I will build My church, and the very gates of hell shall not prevail against it, and whatever you bind on earth shall be bound on heaven, and whatever you loose on earth shall be loosed in heaven" (Matthew16: 18b-19 NIV).

# <u>Casting Down Strongholds</u>

"Everything God builds, He builds on a relational foundation."

Dennis Peacocke

The keys to unlock to the prison doors were given to the church. "Truly, I say to you, whatever you bind on earth shall be bound in heaven, and whatever you loose on earth shall be loosed in heaven. Again I say to you, if two of you agree on earth about anything they ask, it will be done for them by my Father in heaven" (Matthew 18:18-19 ESV). Some of the consequences of prayerlessness and lack of unity we have already seen. There is the power of agreement. Yet, the black church has not collectively come together to address the spiritual roots of our troubles and bondages that still oppress our people some 150 years after slavery. Though there was an Emancipation Declaration issued on paper, the issues of spiritual strongholds have never been collectively dealt with. How could there not be detrimental effects in the lives of black people after being enslaved in excess of 200 years? Have we as a people been in denial? These effects or symptoms have been called "Post Traumatic Slave Disorder" or Syndrome. There is sufficient literature out there to examine the topic, which includes a book entitled: *Breaking the Psychological Chains of Slavery*. The issues are not just psychological.

Cindy Trimm 's book, *The Rules of Engagement: The Art of Strategic Prayer and Spiritual Warfare,* is a most excellent resource on the topic of strongholds. In Part 2: Your Enemy, she expounds on strongholds that must be destroyed.[15] She states, "A stronghold is a pattern and idea that governs individuals, nations and communities. They are mindsets, thoughts, patterns, and processes that cause people to act, react and respond in a particular manner contrary to the ways of God and a godly lifestyle. Strongholds are things that you rationalize and justify. You may say things like, 'My whole family is like this,' 'I can't help it, I was born like this,' 'This is just the way I am,' or 'Everybody acts and thinks this way.' Your rationalization and justification of certain thoughts, behavior, and attitudes form a stronghold.

Strongholds can also be cultural. She goes on to say, "You have to understand that God wants to give you a better way of living and operating in the earth realm. All successful deliverance must begin by first removing that which defends the enemy. In speaking of spiritual warfare, apostle Paul enlists the word *stronghold* to define the spiritual fortresses wherein Satan and his legions hide and are protected. These fortresses exist in the thought patterns and ideas that govern individuals and organizations as well as communities and nations. We must not allow the enemy to

---

[15] Trimm, Cindy, *The Rules of Engagement: The Art of Strategic Prayer and Spiritual Warfare* (Lake Mary: Charisma House), p. 45.

hide himself and his tactics within these fortresses. Every arsenal of the enemy must be removed and replaced with the mighty arsenal of the Word of God."

Apostle Kimberly Daniels explains in her book *Give it back,* "Ephesians 2:2 describes the assignment of the prince of the power of the air. One name for the Greek god of the second heaven is Zeus. The second heaven is the demonic headquarters that is strategically set up to control people like puppets on a string. In the spirit, that is exactly how it looks—likes a puppet show! Every human being is connected to either the second or third heaven. People who are bound by second heaven activity are connected to the second heaven by demonic strings. The hydra is the god of recurring curses and is also seated in the heavens. It is one of the constellations or groups of stars that abide in the heavens. The power of the air (or unconscious cycles is a subliminal bondage, which is controlled from the air. The spirit hides behind the cover of natural habits, and its victims never suspect that they are under its control. Before people are delivered from addictions and habits demonic strings most be cut in the spirit to sever their alliances with the second heaven. After this, ground level deliverance can take place."[16] Thus, we must spiritually discern our atmosphere to understand who is ruling. Then we move to advance the kingdom of God. "Thy Kingdom come, thy will be done" (Matthew 6:10 NIV).

---

[16] Kimberly Daniels, *Give It Back!: God's Weapons for Turning Evil to Good* (Lake Mary: Charisma House), p. 135.

## Identifying and Binding the Strongman

In *The Rules of Engagement* by Cindy Trimm's, her chapter
on "Reconnaissance" exposes the strongman behind slavery. They
are Spirits of Egypt, Pharaoh, and Herod. She includes four pages
in her book of signs, symptoms, and the various manifestations of
these strongholds. All of these manifestations however are
attributed to at least six different types of slavery of which slavery
by descent is only one. She explains, "Slavery by descent is where
people are either born into a slave class or are from a group that
society views as suited to being used as slave labor."[17]

These issues have become spiritual, psychological, emotional
strongholds entrenched in our race. We are instructed in Matthew
12:29 that we must first deal with the strongman: "Or how can one
enter into the house of the strong man, and spoil his goods, except
he first bind the strong man? And then he will spoil his house"
(ASV). We must immobilize the activity of these particular
demonic powers by engaging spiritual warfare strategies, of which
binding and loosing is one. After identifying the ruling powers,
subordinate spirits, we collectively bind them, and then close and
collapse every demonic portal that was opened at the onset of the
enslavement of African Americans. It behooves us, the church of
God, to come out of denial and acknowledge the contributions of

---

[17] Cindy Trimm, The Rules of Engagement (Charisma House, Lake Mary), p.
181.

Deliverance Ministries and work with them to secure not only our own freedom, but also the freedom of our people. They are like "spiritual abolitionists." Harriet Tubman secured her freedom first, and then went back and helped secure the freedom of others. This is an opportunity for the body of Christ to work together as never before. The passage in Ephesians 2:20 states, "Built on the foundation of the apostles and prophets, with Christ Jesus himself as the chief cornerstone. In Him the whole building is joined together and rises to become a holy temple in the Lord" (NIV). We come together under church leadership, working in synergy of unity. This is the way to secure safe passage for our people as they come out of captivity into the Promised Land.

**The Mystery of Names**

*"For the mystery of iniquity doth already work: only he who now letteth will let, until he be taken out of the way. And then shall that Wicked be revealed, whom the Lord shall consume with the spirit of his mouth, and shall destroy with the brightness of his coming"*
(2 Thessalonians 2:7 KJV).

Apostle Hopkins, Founder of Pilgrim's Ministry of Deliverance, understood the nature of this spiritual battle extending from unresolved generational issues. In 2003 he recorded a message entitled "Insight on The Willie Lynch Spirit." He expounded on the methodology Willie Lynch used to control the slave population. He targeted specific strongholds, which are still active in the lives of black people today. Names in the Bible are revealing and contain mysteries. In Genesis 10:6, we find the names of Noah's son Ham and his sons "Cush, Mizraim, Put, and Canaan." Ham or the Hamites, were located in southwestern Asia and northeast Africa. Cush, means, "black." The Greek name for Cush is "Ethiopia," which also means blackness or heat. Canaan means, "traffic," as in "moved along" in a transportation system. 'Put' means "Warrior," and 'Mizraim' means Egypt. Embedded in their names are mysteries.

There is a myth that has long circulated about Noah cursing Ham because Ham looked upon his father's nakedness while he was drunk. This had become the justification or rationale for the enslavement of black people. However, his father, Ham, did not curse Cush, from whom black people descended. The Bible passage states, "And Noah said, "Cursed are Canaan! A slave of slaves, a slave to his brothers!" (Genesis 9:25 NIV).

Slavery was purely and simply about profits. Willie Lynch's method's entailed instilling fear, perpetual distrust, and envy in order to control black slaves. Differences were magnified to pit slaves against each other. Differences such as light skin verses dark skinned, straight hair verses nappy hair, house slave verses field slaves. These were strategies for control purposes, which came with a guarantee to last for 300 years until today. It's common to hear a black person say about black people, "I don't know why black people can't get together?

# <u>Let My People Go</u>

*"This is what the Lord Almighty says: "The people of Israel are oppressed, and the people of Judah as well. All their captors hold them fast, refusing to let them go. Yet their Redeemer is strong; the Lord Almighty is His name. He will vigorously defend their cause so that He may bring rest to their land"*

(Jeremiah 50:33 NIV).

*"For it shall come to pass in that day, saith the LORD of hosts, that I will break his yoke from off thy neck, and will burst thy bonds, and strangers shall no more serve themselves of him But they shall serve the LORD their God, and David their king, whom I will raise up unto them"*

(Jeremiah 30:8-9 KJV)

*"Because he loved your fathers, therefore he chose their offspring after them, and brought you out with his presence, with his great power, out of Egypt"*
(Deuteronomy 4:37 WEB).

Cindy Trimm suggests what is needed for a release: The Hand of God, divine visitations, God's mercy, national revival, and the spirit of truth, salvation and deliverance.[18] I appreciate the work that Apostle Kimberly Daniels ,Cindy Trim and Apostle Hopkins have done. God has given them revelatory insight into what is needed to secure freedom.

## Let Freedom Reign

The prophetic freedom song, at the vanguard, has already been released into the atmosphere. It is the new freedom song for our generation. It speaks of the power of God to do what He wants to do. "There is power in the name of Jesus, to break every chain, break every chain. We don't just see the chains failing, but we hear and feel the chains falling."[19] It is a prophetic declaration of a movement in the Spirit. The Bible says in Zechariah 4:6, "Not by might nor by power, but by My Spirit, says the Lord of Hosts" (NIV). It is the spiritual forces of darkness that must first be dealt with. In Ephesians chapter 6 Paul describes the nature of the true and invisible battle:

"For our wrestling is not against flesh and blood, but against the principalities, against the powers, against the world's rulers of the darkness of this age, and against the spiritual

---

[18] Cindy Trimm, *The Rules of Engagement* (Charisma House, Lake Mary).
[19] *Break Every Chain*, Tasha Cobbs, *Grace* (2013 AllMusic Rovi Corporation).

forces of wickedness in the heavenly places. [13]Therefore put on the whole armor of God,that you may be able to withstand in the evil day, and having done all, to stand. [14]Stand therefore, having the utility belt of truth buckled around your waist, and having put on the breastplate of righteousness, [15]and having fitted your feet with the preparation of the Good News of peace, [16]above all, taking up the shield of faith, with which you will be able to quench all the fiery darts of the evil one. [17]And take the helmet of salvation, and the sword of the Spirit, which is the word of God" (6:12-17 WEB).

The previously mentioned issues with respect to African Americans, including the mass incarceration of black males, are the 'fruits' of prayerlessness. There is more that is required from the church than business as usual. In Mark 9: 28-29 it says, "Then, after he went into the house, his disciples asked him privately, 'Why couldn't we cast it out?' He told them, 'This kind can come out only by prayer'" (NET). It is here where we need the guidance of the Holy Spirit. We need to fervently seek out His illumination, spirit-led revelation and discernment to effectively engage the enemies of our souls. This has been an ungodly slumber, maybe brought on by the stress and magnitude of the issues facing us. Yet, while the church sleeps, the storm rages on. Nonetheless, God has raised up culturally prophetic voices through which He continues to deliver a message to the generations.

**State of Emergency**

In 1968, Baltimore, Maryland had sub-par housing, increased crime, and black unemployment was double. Governor Agnew declared a state of emergency.

In 1975, Teddy Pendergrass came out with a featured selection on an album by Harold Melvin and the Bluenotes. The selection was called "Wake Up Everybody"

> *Wake up everybody no more sleepin' in bed*
> *No more backward thinkin' time for thinkin' ahead*
> *The world has changed so very much*
> *From what it used to be*
> *There is so much hatred war and poverty.*[20]

In 1978, Nina Simeone came out with an album entitled "Oh, Baltimore." She sang,

"Hard times in the city. In a hard town by the sea. Ain't nowhere to run to. There ain't nothin' here for free. Hard times in the city. In a hard town by the sea. Ain't nowhere to run to. There ain't nothin' here for free…Oh, Baltimore Man, it's hard just to live. Oh, Baltimore Man, it's hard just to live, just to live."[21]

---

[20] Victor Carstaphen, Gene Mcfadden, John Whitehead, Wake Up Everybody, (Warner-tamerlane Publishing) Harold Melvin & the Blue Notes version, 1976.
[21] "Baltimore" was composed by Randy Newman and originally appeared on his 1977 album *Little Criminals*.

On that same album, she recorded a selection about the family entitled "Looks like only God can save the family." That was in 1978. Fast Forward to August 9, 2014, another state of emergency was called in Ferguson Missouri, due to civil unrest. Michael Brown, an 18-year-old black man was fatally shot by a white police officer. Michael Brown was unarmed. Fast forward to Baltimore in 2015, where another "State of emergency" is called because of protests due to the hospitalization and subsequent death of Freddie Gray. He died while in police custody. Protestors demonstrated at the Baltimore Police Department Western District Building. Approximately 250 people were arrested and thousands of Maryland Army National Guards were deployed.

June 2015 in Charleston, North Carolina, there was the senseless massacre of nine innocent black people attending a prayer meeting at Emanuel AME, an historic African American church. A young 21-year-old white man went on a rampage because of his racist beliefs. He is quoted as saying, " You rape our women and you're taking over our country."

**Where does the madness end?**

Then, there is the issue of the mass incarceration of black men, which is exacting a heavy toll upon African Americans. We, as a people, are and have been in a state of emergency. As you can see, there are many ongoing examples of the unspeakable that will not stop until we decide to take action together.

# You, Son of Man are the Watchman

*"For thus hath the Lord said unto me, Go, set a watchman: let him declare what he seeth"* (Isaiah 21:6 ASV)

*"Set up the standard upon the walls of Babylon, make the watch strong, set up the watchmen, prepare the ambushes"* (Jeremiah 51:12b KJV)

Ezekiel 33:1-5 declares: "The word of the Lord came to me: 'Son of man, speak to your people, and say to them, 'Suppose I bring a sword against the land, and the people of the land take one man from their borders and make him their watchman. He sees the sword coming against the land, blow the trumpet, and warns the people, but there is one who hears the sound of the trumpet yet does not heed the warning. Then the sword comes and sweeps him away. He will be responsible for his own death. He heard the sound of the trumpet but did not heed the warning, so he is responsible for himself. If he had heeded the warning, he would have saved his life" (NET)

Verses 6-9 continue: "But suppose the watchman sees the sword coming and does not blow the trumpet to warn the people. Then the sword come and takes one of their lives. He is swept away for his iniquity, but I will hold the watchman accountable for that person's death.' "As for you, son of man, I have made you a watchman for the house of Israel. Whenever you hear a word from my mouth, you must warn them on my behalf. When I say to the wicked, 'O wicked man, you must certainly die,' and you do not warn the wicked about his behavior, the wicked man will die for his iniquity, but I will hold you accountable for his death. But if you warn the wicked man to change his behavior, and he refuses to change, he will die for his iniquity, but you have saved your own life"

It is time for the watchman to wake up and assume their positions on the wall. To pray without ceasing, until the chains of slavery have been broken, and the bondage of slavery has been disarmed, dismantled, and dismayed. It is time for the African American people to Passover from bondage to freedom. God's message to Cyrus:

"This is what the Lord says to his chosen one,

to Cyrus, whose right hand I hold

in order to subdue nations before him,

and disarm kings,

to open doors before him,

so gates remain unclosed:

"I will go before you

and level mountains.

Bronze doors I will shatter

and iron bars I will hack through.

I will give you hidden treasures,

riches stashed away in secret places,

so you may recognize that I am the Lord,

the one who calls you by name the God of Israel.

For the sake of my servant Jacob,

Israel, my chosen one,

I call you by name

and give you a title of respect, even though you do not

recognize [7]me.

I am the Lord, I have no peer,

there is no God but me.

I arm you for battle, even though you do not recognize me.

I do this so people will recognize from east to west

That there is no God but me;

I am the Lord, I have no peer.

I am the one who form light

and creates darkness;

the one who brings about peace

and creates calamity.

I am the Lord, who accomplishes all these things" (Isaiah
45:1-7 NET)

Then Isaiah finishes with these words of heartfelt prayer:

"O sky, rain down from above!

Let the clouds send down showers of deliverance!

Let the earth absorb it so salvation may grow,

and deliverance may sprout up along with it.

I, the Lord, create it" (Verse 8).


May it be so today for whole church.


## Exodus
## "I'm Coming Out"
Diana Ross


*"And Moses said unto the people, Fear ye not, stand still, and see the salvation of the Lord, which he will shew to you today: for the Egyptians whom ye have seen today, ye shall see them again no more forever."*

(Exodus 14:1 KJV)


*The Year of the Lord's Favor*

*"The Spirit of the Sovereign Lord is on me, because the Lord has anointed me to proclaim good news to the poor. He has sent me to bind up the brokenhearted, to proclaim freedom for the captives and release from darkness for the prisoners, to proclaim the year of the Lord's favor and the day of vengeance of our God, to comfort all who mourn, and provide for those who grieve in Zion— to bestow on them a crown of beauty instead of ashes, the oil of joy instead of mourning, and a garment of praise instead of a spirit of despair. They will be called oaks of righteousness, a planting of*

*the Lord for the display of his splendor. They will rebuild the ancient ruins and restore the places long devastated; they will renew the ruined cities that have been devastated for generations"*
(Isaiah 61:1-5 KJV)

The children of Israel were in oppressive bondage for at least two-hundred-years, but God brought them out, and I expect Him to do the same for us as a people. Collectively in the Spirit, we declare to the principalities, powers, and dominions "Let my people go" until their freedom is secured. Fifteen years ago I attempted to mobilize local intercessors to pray for African Americans. I started a prayer group called Intercessors For African–Americans. Sadly, it dissolved due to lack of participation. A little later I attempted to bring it back as Intercessors For The African Diaspora. I didn't give up easily. I sent out prayer cards to different churches requesting that they pray the prayer focus written on the cards. After not receiving feedback or encouragement, along with the cost of printing the postcards, I threw in the towel. Occasionally someone would say, "that's good," but nobody wanted to invest their time or 'sweat equity' into praying for us. The vision was not there, and we were just not important enough to pray for.

Well, history belongs to the intercessors for good or for bad. What can the church say now? The kids had a saying when they didn't do something they should have, "My bad!" That's about what we should be saying to God right now. I muse whether or not it was symptomatic of 'post traumatic slave syndrome.'"

My friend and mentor, Rev. Amos, director of a missions' organizations, told me several years after my experience that there was no national 'black prayer movement' in this country and suggested the need to mobilize as intercessors and function as one entity. He said, "It is then that things will change." What he said resonated within me, and it confirmed that I had indeed been on the right track. It is clear now that a correlation exists between our failure to mobilize and the present state of our race. As stated previously, the impact of posttraumatic slave syndrome and the spiritual strongholds have impacted the church to the extent that we fail to see our need to mobilize in prayer. But, as the old song says, there is a Balm in Gilead that heals the wounded soul. In Hebrews12:12 we are admonished "Therefore strengthen the hands which hang down, and make straight paths for your feet, so that what is lame may not be put out of joint but be healed" (NET). This is a crucial juncture for the black church and could be one of our finest hours. But we must unite together and avail ourselves as God's instrument to usher our people out of oppressive bondage into freedom. It is once again time for an exodus. In Jeremiah 51:20, the Lord of Hosts says, "You are my battle-axe and weapons of war. For with you I will break the nation in pieces. With you I will destroy kingdoms" (KJV). First we root out, and then pull down, next we destroy and throw down. In Jeremiah 1:9 it states, "Behold, I have put my words in your mouth, See I have set you over the nations and over kingdoms. To root out, and to pull down, to destroy and to throw down to build and to plant" (KJV). We are engaged in a spiritual battle "For though we live in the world, we do not wage war as the world does" (2 Corinthians 10:3 NIV). The weapons we fight with are not the weapons of the world. On the contrary, our weapons have divine power to demolish strongholds. We demolish arguments and every pretension that sets itself up against the knowledge of God, and we take captive every thought to make it obedient to Christ (2 Corinthians 10:4-5). The kingdom of Heaven suffers violence, and the violent take it by force.

After we have uprooted and pulled down the demonic strongholds holding our people hostage, then we are to build up and plant. We sow the seed of God's word. James 1:21b says.... "and receive with meekness the engrafted word, which is able to save your souls" (KJV). We prophetically decree and declare God's word over our lives. We speak as an oracle of God. We incubate and give birth to the promises of God. Our attitude must be 'I will not let you go until you bless me' as demonstrated in the story of Jacob. The passage states "Jacob was left alone, and a man wrestled with him until daybreak. When he saw that he not prevailed against him, he touched the socket of his thigh; so the socket of Jacob's thigh was dislocated while he wrestled with him. Then he said," Let me go, for the dawn is breaking "But he said, "I will not let you go unless you bless me"(Genesis 32:24-26 NIV). It is a spiritual tenacity, a wrestling match to take back what belongs to us. So we all work together to wrestle, to labor, to give birth to a new movement of God. We are impregnated with the seed of God's word. We visualize this birthing process found in Isaiah 66:8 "Who has heard such a thing? Who has seen such a thing? Can a land be born in a day? Can a nation be brought forth all at once? "As soon Zion travailed, she also brought forth her sons" (KJV). Paul says in Galatians 4:19 "My children--I am again undergoing birth pains until Christ is formed in you!" (NET).

The passage in Job 22:28 states "You shall also decree a thing, and it shall be established to you. Light shall shine on your ways" (WEB). We do this in the strength of the Lord of Hosts. In Isaiah 58:6 God is portrayed as "a spirit of justice and a source of strength to those who turn back the battle at the gate." And in Deuteronomy 4:37, it is stated that He brought them out of Egypt with "His Presence and mighty power." God will bring us out of Egypt with His presence and in His power if only we will pray.

## "Papa's Got a Brand New Bag"

James Brown

A Time of Visitation: A New Season, A New Work

*"From now on I will tell you of new things, of hidden things unknown to you. They are created now, and not from long ago; they are created now, and not long ago; you have not heard of them before today. So you cannot say, Yes, I knew them. You have neither heard nor understood"*

(Isaiah 48:6b, 7 NIV).

*"And new things I declare: Before they spring forth I tell you of them"*
(Isaiah 42:9b NIV)

"Papa God" has a plan for us, described in Jeremiah 29:11-13, "For I know the plans I towards you, says the Lord, thoughts of peace and not of evil, to give you a future and a hope. Then you will call upon me and go and pray to me, and I will listen to you. And You will find me when you search for me with all of your heart" (NIV). God discloses His plan through His prophet

Jeremiah. Part of the plan is to free the captives. Here's another "nugget" for you. In Jeremiah 30:8-10 God says, "For it shall come to pass in that day, Says the Lord of Hosts, "that I will break his yoke from your neck, And will burst your bonds; Foreigners shall no more enslave them. But they shall serve the Lord their God..." (CLB). It is important to know the times and seasons. The passage in Ecclesiastes says there is a time for everything, and a season for every activity under the heavens. After the mystery was revealed to Daniel he praised God and said, "Blessed be the name of God for ever and ever: for wisdom and might are his" (Daniel 2:20 KJV). Daniel went on to say that God changes times and seasons, and he deposes kings while raising up others. God gives wisdom to the wise and knowledge to the discerning, revealing deep and hidden things. Daniel declared that God knows what lies in darkness, and that light dwells with Him. Brothers and Sister, the seasons have changed.

This is a new season of open doors. It is a time were the door for deliverance from historic and prolonged trauma; the entrenched evil of generational slavery can be closed. It is a time to cut off the influences of past oppressions and to move forward as the liberated children of God. We move out of slavery and step into the Promised Land, or the land of promises. We reclaim, recapture and possess our spiritual identity as sons and daughters of God and a spiritual inheritance of blessings. It is a time to "Look up" for our redemption draws near (Luke 21:28). There are prophets who have declared that this is the "Year of the Open Door." We need to take a collective step forward as the Body of Christ into that door. Doors are symbolic of seasons and opportunities. In this is new season for deliverance and restoration, God promises that when He refreshes the land, he will restore those lost years. In Joel it states, "I will restore to you the years that the swarming locusts has eaten. The crawling locust. The consuming locusts and the chewing locusts" (2:25 CLB). This is a new door. God says in Isaiah that He's doing new things. "You have heard; now look at all the evidence! Will you not admit that what I say is true? From this point on I am announcing to you new events that are previously unrevealed and you do not know about" (Isaiah 48:6 NET). This is a new work of the Spirit of God, so "Get on board, little children."

As a body, we need to cross over the threshold. The "new" has arrived. For God will pour water on our thirsty land, and he will spread streams on our dry ground. God will indeed pour out His Spirit on your offspring and mine, and His blessings will be on our descendants and they will spring up like grass in a meadow. Like poplar trees they will once again grow flowing streams. And our people will say, 'I belong to the LORD.' (Isaiah 44:3–5). This is the Lord's promise.

This is a season of great hope and expectation. We declare Jubilee and the year of the Lord's favor. God has neither forsaken nor forgotten us. Indeed, this is what the Lord says: "Refrain your voice from weeping, and your eyes from tears; for your work shall be rewarded, says Yahweh; and they shall come again from the land of the enemy. There is hope for your latter end, says Yahweh;

and [your] children shall come again to their own border"
(Jeremiah 31:16–17 WEB).

# Pray Together Children: Don't You Get Weary:

## The Spiritual Imperative for This Generation

*"Also in Judah the hand of God was on the people to give them unity of mind to carry out what the king and his officials had ordered, following the word of the Lord"*
(2 Chronicles 30:12 NIV)

*"And the Lord said "Behold, the people is one, and they have all one language; and they begin to do: and now nothing will be restrained from them, which they have imagined to do"*
(Genesis 11:6 KJV)

*"But with one accord they too had broken off the yoke and torn off the bonds"*
(Jeremiah 5:5 NIV).

## The Power of Agreement

*"Though one may be overpowered, two can defend themselves. A*
*cord of three strands is not quickly broken"*
(Ecclesiastes 4:12 NIV)

Kimberly Daniels addressed the need for collective intercession in 2007 in her book, *Give it Back*. She stated, " Over the years there have been many great moves of God. The move that we need to get our stuff out of the enemy's camp is corporate prayer revival. It is time for the dead bones of the church to stand up and thrive in intercession and warfare. Wow! Ezekiel prophesied to dead bones, and they did not just come alive, they became a great army."[22]

We must not only pray, but we must pray together, functioning as a healthy body. In Matthew 18:19 it says, "Again I say unto you if two of you agree on anything that they ask, it will be done for them by My father in Heaven" (NKJ). Jesus desired the church to function in perfect unity. He stated in John 17:21-23 "that they may all be one; even as you, Father, are in me, and I in you, that they also may be one in us; that the world may believe that you sent me" (WEB).

In the article, "History Belongs to the Intercessors" by Walter Wink[23], intercession is described as the interior battlefield where

---

[22] Kimberly Daniels, *Give It Back!: God's Weapons for Turning Evil to Good* (Lake Mary: Charisma House), p. 66.
[23] Excerpted from *Engaging the Powers* published by Fortress Press, USA

the intercessor is not bound to the status quo. In whatever form the oppression is manifested, and from whence ever it comes, intercession remains the instrument to break and demolish the yoke. Intercession in the Bible is rooted in the assumption that the prayer of faith rules over anything this worldly system can offer. In the Book of Ezra, we see another example of what God did when His people united together in corporate prayer, undergirded with fasting. In Ezra 8:21-23, it states the following, "Then I proclaimed a fast there, at the river Ahava, that we might humble ourselves before our God, to seek of him a straight way for us, and for our little ones, and for all our substance. For I was ashamed to ask of the king a band of soldiers and horsemen to help us against the enemy in the way, because we had spoken to the king, saying, 'The hand of our God is on all those who seek him, for good; but his power and his wrath is against all those who forsake him.' So we fasted and begged our God for this: and he was entreated of us" (WEB). Ezra was ashamed to ask the king for his help, conscious of the claims that he made concerning His God. Instead, Ezra humbled himself and called for a corporate fast. Unlike Ezra, we have not sought God in the right way, for our children, our race, and ourselves. As a result our own children have become victims in a culture where violence has been magnified in music, video games, and movies—and has reached epidemic proportions. In Los Angeles teenagers were planning their own funerals, motivated out of fear that they would fall prey to gang warfare. Like never before we need to heed Ezra's example and come together with the goal of seeking the God who created heaven and earth. The future and destiny of generations are hanging in the balance. In the New Testament Book of Acts, we find another scenario in which corporate prayer was the decisive factor in the final outcome. In Acts, Chapter 12, the saints in Jerusalem united together and earnestly prayed for Peter. Act 12:15 states "So Peter was kept in prison, but the church was earnestly praying to God for him" (NIV) In verse 6 and 7, we see how God miraculously answered their prayers. "The same night when Herod was about to bring him out, Peter was sleeping between two soldiers, bound with two chains. Guards in front of the door kept the prison. ⁷And behold, an angel of the Lord stood by him, and a light shone in the cell. He struck Peter on the side, and woke him up, saying, "Stand up quickly!" His chains fell off from his hands" (WEB)

Then the angel told him to get up and put on your clothes and sandals, and Peter did so. He told him to wrap his cloak around himself and to follow him. So Peter followed him out of the prison but had no idea that what the angel was doing because he thought he was seeing things. When they came to the Iron Gate leading to the city, it opened for them by itself and they went through it. Peter acknowledged, " Now I know for certain that the Lord has sent his angel and rescued me from the hand of Herod and from everything the Jewish people were expecting to happen" (Acts 12:11 NET). God's people who are called by His Name, humbled with corporate fasting and prayer, sought God and were answered. We are encouraged in Romans 6:9 to not grow weary in well doing, for in due season, we will reap a harvest if we faint not.

God is raising up those who will stand in the gap. The effectual and fervent prayer of the righteous man availeth much, according to James 5:16. God is bringing restoration to intercessory prayer in the last days, especially in America! Out of this intercessory prayer movement, prayer warriors will be birthed. Fervent, aggressive, unrelenting prayer is the foundation upon which the walls will be rebuilt.

# <u>Sing Together Children: Don't You Get Weary</u>

## A "New Song" for a New Movement

*"Blessed are the people who know the joyful sound"*
(Psalm 89:15 KJV).
*"…The season of singing has come…"*
(Song of Songs 2: 12b NIV).
*"I will sing of Your love and Your Justice"*
(Psalm101: 1 NIV).
*"The singers went before, the players on the instruments followed*
*after; among them were the maidens playing timbrels"*
(Psalm 68: 25 CLB).
*"But now bring me a minstrel". And it came to pass, when the*
*minstrel played, that the hand of the Lord came upon him"*
(2 Kings 3:15 KJV).
*"Your watchmen shall lift up their voices. With their voices they*
*shall sing together. For they shall see eye to eye"*
(Isaiah 52:8 CLB).

It's been stated that every new movement is preceded by a sound. In the book, *The Physics of Heaven* written by Ray Hughes, there is a chapter written on the sound of Heaven: the Symphony of the Earth. Hughes posits that music is an indicator. "Throughout the generations of history, the spiritual climate of God's people has responded to a musical indicator. With every revival there has been a release of a new music or a new sound. Whether the music releases revival, or whether the revival releases the music, varies from generation to generation. However, the sound changes as God's people respond to what God is doing or saying"[24]

Previously, we looked at the story of Jehoshaphat in 2 Chronicles. The people came together to pray, but as a part of that prayer they also did something else significant. They set what Watchman Nee refers to in his book entitled, *The Overcoming Life,* as the 'tone for victory.'[25] In 2 Chronicles, chapter 20:21, it reads "He met with the people and appointed musicians to play before the LORD and praise his majestic splendor. As they marched ahead of the warriors they said: "Give thanks to the LORD, for his loyal love endures" (NET). The singers and the musicians were sent ahead of the soldiers to the front lines of the battle. As they began to sing and praise, the Lord set ambushes.

Music will once again lead as we enter a new phase in this very strategic warfare for the souls of our people. As the praises of God were sung, the enemies of Judah and Jerusalem were defeated. When the men of Judah came to the place that overlooks the desert

[24] Ray Hughes, The Physics of Heaven, (Fort Mill SC, Morningstar Publications, 2000), P.69.
[25] Watchman Nee, *The Overcoming Life,* (Anaheim, CA, Living Stream Ministry) 1 edition 1997.

and looked toward that vast army, they only saw dead bodies lying on the ground: no one escaped.[26] In verses 26-28 it continues: "On the fourth day they assembled in the Valley of Berachah, where they praised the LORD. So that place is called the Valley of Berachah to this very day. Then all the men of Judah and Jerusalem returned joyfully to Jerusalem with Jehoshaphat leading them; the LORD had given them reason to rejoice over their enemies. They entered Jerusalem to the sound of stringed instruments and trumpets and proceeded to the temple of the LORD" (NET)

In Psalms 100:4, it tells us to enter God's gates with thanksgiving and into His courts with praise. That is the "Tone of Victory," before the battle, and after the battle is over. Here is an example of sound preceding movement. During the Abolitionist Movement, which reached its peak in the 1840-1850, music was key and proved very powerful. William Wells Brown, a former slave, published the anti-slavery Harp, which was a collection of songs. Likewise, Guy Carawan has called the music of the Civil Rights Era the greatest singing movement this country has ever experienced. We are right to acknowledge and to honor African-American history with its rich and many contributions. During the Abolitionist Era and the Civil Rights Era, the music provided a powerful voice for the disenfranchised, for social and racial justice and equality. The music also served to encourage the weary and to

---

[26] Ibid. p.155.

mobilize the people. Even then, during the Civil rights Era those songs were only a "new song" in that they were adaptations of traditional hymns and Negro spirituals infused with new lyrics, which addressed the issues of their day. "We Shall Overcome" unofficially became the anthem for the movement. Song and music became central to the struggle for freedom. Martin Luther King, Jr. attested to this during the Albany Movement. He said, "They gave the people courage and a sense of unity. I think they keep alive a faith, a radiant hope in the future, particularly in our most trying hours."

In the 1961 Freedom Rides songs played a critical role in sustaining morale for those serving time in the Mississippi's Hinds County jail. James Farmer, National Director of the Congress of Racial Equality (CORE), and a Freedom Ride participant, recalled one night when a voice called out from the cell block to the freedom riders: Sing your freedom song. We sang old folk songs and the gospel messages to which new words had been written, telling of the Freedom Ride and its purpose. The female freedom riders in another wing of the jail joined in, and for the first time in history, the Hinds County jail rocked with unrestrained singing of songs about freedom and brotherhood.[27] Once again we see in history a sound and a movement. We need ears that are tuned into the frequency and sound waves of heaven, that we may hear the "new song." The song for the moment that we are living in. Let us synchronize with the third heaven, listening for the release of the

---

[27] James Leonard Farmer, Jr. (January 12, 1920 – July 9, 1999).

new sound that can obliterate strongholds and cause them to come falling down like the walls of Jericho. Can you hear the song?

# People Get Ready, There's a "Rain a Comin'

One of my former pastors, Apostle Robinson, preached a powerful message on pain one Sunday morning. He spoke of personal pain and the corporate pain of slavery. He made a statement that I have never forgotten. I referred earlier to culturally prophetic voices. He said that we as a people have not been without cultural prophets in our time. However, the cultural prophets themselves had been broken by the weight of their own personal pain, which they could not carry. Curtis Mayfield was also one such prophet, although there have been many others. Curtis Mayfield's song "People Get Ready"[28] was and remains prophetic. The song gets right to the heart of the gospel message. God uses Curtis Mayfield and many others to find those who might not ordinarily find their way to a church. He was used to give voice to an admonition and for encouragement.

People get ready. Get ready for what? Get ready for an appointed destination on the train on the journey of life. One day it will stop at your destination, the appointed destiny of all mankind is to appear and give an account before the Sovereign Almighty

---

[28] Curtis Mayfield, "People Get Ready" 1965 single from the *People Get Ready* album, ABC Paramount.

God, the Creator and Ruler of all existence. Now is the time to prepare. A new wave of song is emerging and as Curtis Mayfield, wrote, "People get ready. The music shall be and is at the vanguard of a new and fresh move of the Lord. Get ready for a fresh visitation and outpouring of the Holy Spirit. There is yet another """ of revival on the horizon. Acts 2:16-17 states "And it shall come to pass in the last days, saith God, I will pour out of my Spirit upon all flesh: and your sons and your daughters shall prophesy, and your young men shall see visions, and your old men shall dream dreams" (KJV). The exact same promise was given in the Old Testament Book of Joel, chapter 2:28-29 "It will happen afterward, that I will pour out my Spirit on all flesh; and your sons and your daughters will prophesy. Your old men will dream dreams. Your young men will see visions. And also on the servants and on the handmaids in those days, I will pour out my Spirit" (WEB).

Once again there is a sound, it is the sound of the rain of God being poured out in abundance. God asks Job in chapter 38:37 "Who has the wisdom to count the clouds? Who can tip over the water jars of heaven, when the dust becomes hard and the clods of earth stick together? Have we "the dust" become hard towards God? What do we need? We need God to tip over the water jars of heaven and rain down the mercy of God upon our dust'" (NIV). "For there is hope for a tree, if it is cut down, that it will sprout again, and that its tender shoots will not cease. Though its roots may grow old in the earth, and its stump may die in the ground, yet at the scent of water it will bud and bring forth branches like a plant" (Job 14:7-9 NIV) People get ready for the rain.

The prophet Hosea admonishes us, "Break up your fallow ground, for it is time to seek the Lord, till He comes and rains down righteousness on you" (Hos 10:12 NIV). Fallow ground is the type of ground that Job referred to, hardened ground that for a time remained dormant. That hard ground needs to be plowed and cultivated. Fix your *eyes and ears* on Jesus so you can see when the clouds of revival begin to form. And hear the sound of the rain. Stand in the rain and allow yourself to get wet. Remember in Exodus 13:21, God led the children of Israel by a cloud by day. In 11 Chronicles 5:12-14 all the Levites who were musicians— Asaph, Heman, Jeduthun and their sons and relatives—stood on the east side of the altar, dressed in fine linen and playing cymbals, harps and lyres. One hundred and twenty priests sounding trumpets accompanied them. The trumpeters and the singers joined in unison, as with one voice, to give praise and thanks to the Lord.

The Amplified Bible says, "This is the beginning of what was spoken through the prophet Joel: and it shall come to pass in the last days, God says that I will pour out My Spirit upon all mankind...." (Joel 2:28). We need to open the gates of revival with thanksgiving and praise. Creating the atmosphere for the presence and power of God. In 1910, in the Pentecostal outpouring at Azusa Street, William Seymour prophesied that in 100 years there would be a release of God's Shekinah Glory that would exceed the power of what occurred during the Azusa Street revival. The prophetic promises that have been dormant are now beginning to activate.

Ruth Heflin was an author of many books about the glory of God. In her book, River Glory, she wrote the following "There is something about the new song that brings a release in ways that nothing else can. The move of the Spirit of God comes on the wings of song, and as some of you release your song to the Lord you will find yourself flowing in a new dimension of the Spirit, in a new realm of the Spirit, moving in a new place in God. God is ready to bring forth the new song, but we must cooperate with Him.[29] There is music and singing and a new song to be played and sung in the river"[30] Zephaniah 3:14-17 says this: "Sing, daughter of Zion! Shout, Israel! Be glad and rejoice with all your heart, daughter of Jerusalem. Yahweh has taken away your judgments. He has thrown out your enemy. The King of Israel, Yahweh, is in the midst of you. You will not be afraid of evil any more. In that day, it will be said to Jerusalem, "Don't be afraid, Zion. Don't let your hands be weak." Yahweh, your God, is in the midst of you, a mighty one who will save. He will rejoice over you with joy. He will calm you in his love. He will rejoice over you with singing" (WEB). Ruth Heflin declared for years that the revival that is coming would be a singing revival. That the songs would come

---

[29] Ruth Hefflin, River Glory, McDougal Publishing Company (February 1, 1999), p. 249.
[30] Ibid. p. 250.

fresh from the God's very throne room. She also stated "The power is not in the voice, it is in the river."[31]

---

[31] Ibid. p. 257.

# I Have a Dream

*"Your old men shall dream, dreams"*
(Joel 2:28 )

*"Now Joseph had a dream, and he told it to his brothers, and they
hated him even more"* (Genesis 37:5 CLB)

*"Therefore judge nothing before the appointed time; wait until the
Lord comes"*
(1 Corinthians 4:5 NIV)

*"So the wall was finished in the twenty and fifth day of the month
Elul, in fifty and two days"*
(Nehemiah 6:15 KJV)

Fifty-two years ago on August 28, 1963, two hundred and fifty
thousand people converged upon the Washington National Mall.
They came to hear Dr. Martin Luther King Jr. give what has
become an historic address "I Have A Dream." It was a dream of
freedom and equality for all. God gives and communicates through
dreams. Some examples of Biblical dreamers are Joseph, Daniel,
Habakkuk, Obadiah, Abraham, Nahum, Peter, and Paul.

I am a part of a corporate company of dreamers who dream also of restoration like that described in Psalm 126, also called A Song of Ascents:

> When the LORD restored the well-being of Zion,
>
> we thought we were dreaming.
>
> At that time we laughed loudly
>
> and shouted for joy.
>
> At that time the nations said,
>
> "The LORD has accomplished great things for these people."
>
> The LORD did indeed accomplish great things for us.
>
> We were happy.
>
> O LORD, restore our well-being,
>
> just as the streams in the arid south are replenished.
>
> Those who shed tears as they plant
>
> will shout for joy when they reap the harvest.
>
> The one who weeps as he walks along, carrying his bag of seed,
>
> will certainly come in with a shout of joy, carrying his sheaves of grain" (NET).

I see it as a vision of our future. Psalm 129 is a song of victory over the enemies of our souls.

> "Since my youth they have often attacked me,"
>
> let Israel say.
>
> "Since my youth they have often attacked me,

but they have not defeated me.

The plowers plowed my back;

they made their furrows long.

The LORD is just;

he cut the ropes of the wicked."

May all who hate Zion

be humiliated and turned back!

May they be like the grass on the rooftops

which withers before one can even pull it up,

which cannot fill the reaper's hand,

or the lap of the one who gathers the grain!

Those who pass by will not say,

"May you experience the LORD's blessing!

We pronounce a blessing on you in the name of the LORD"

(NET)

# Hope Reformation

*"...weeping may endure for the night, but Joy cometh in the*
*morning"*
(Psalm 30:5 NKJV)

*"Now hope does not disappoint..."*
(Romans 5:5 NKJV)

*"Therefore I am now going to allure her; I will lead her into the*
*wilderness and speak tenderly to her. There I will give her back*
*her vineyards, and will make the Valley of Achor a door of hope"*
(Hosea 2:14-15 NIV)

As we commemorate the anniversary of Dr. King's famous address, racial injustice remains front and center in America. Some have become disillusioned, abandoning all hope for justice and change.

However, the Bible says, "And when these things begin to come to pass, then look up, and lift up your heads; for your redemption draweth nigh" (Luke 21:23 KJV). The time has come for us to gather together binding ourselves vertically and horizontally to a collective hope, a confident steady expectation of good. A hope that transcends this temporal world. "For I know the plans I have for you," declares the Lord, "plans to prosper you and not to harm you, plans to give you hope and a future" (Jeremiah 29:11 NIV). God has big plans for us as a people.

# <u>The Church Triumphant</u>

## Ain't No Stopping Us Now

McFadden and Whitehead

I had another dream, recently. I inquired of God, how to end this message. I waited on God for an impression, a word. After waiting awhile, I saw the base of a tower. I waited again, then I heard "the word": "Walk around Zion, go around her, count her towers." It was an encouraging word full of hope. I read Psalm 48:1-14 in which the verse is found. After I read it I rejoiced again.

## A Psalm of the Sons of Korah

"The LORD is great and certainly worthy of praise

in the city of our God, his holy hill.

It is lofty and pleasing to look at,

a source of joy to the whole earth.

Mount Zion resembles the peaks of Zaphon;

it is the city of the great king.

God is in its fortresses;

he reveals himself as its defender.

For look, the kings assemble;

they advance together.

As soon as they see, they are shocked;

they are terrified, they quickly retreat.

Look at them shake uncontrollably,

like a woman writhing in childbirth.

With an east wind

you shatter the large ships.

We heard about God's mighty deeds, now we have seen them,

in the city of the LORD, the invincible Warrior,

in the city of our God.

God makes it permanently secure. (Selah)

We reflect on your loyal love, O God,

within your temple.

The praise you receive as far away as the ends of the earth

is worthy of your reputation, O God.

You execute justice!

Mount Zion rejoices;

the towns of Judah are happy,

because of your acts of judgment.

Walk around Zion! Encircle it!

Count its towers!

Consider its defenses!

Walk through its fortresses,

so you can tell the next generation about it!

For God, our God, is our defender forever!

He guides us!" (NET)

The Psalmist set the tone for victory by sending "praise" first for God's greatness and goodness. The honor spoken concerning the church is the honor due to our God—for who He is and what He has done. Mount Zion is the city of the great King and is admired for its beauty and "The joy of whole earth." This is the city of which God has chosen to place his name. It is the residence of His grace, and out of his relationship to her flows God's providential care. This Psalm is a vision of the church triumphant, which strikes fear upon their enemies. "Holiness to the Lord" is inscribed upon it, as it was also inscribed upon the High Priest in the Old Testament. The church is a "holy nation, a royal priesthood, a peculiar nation." The temple was built in Mount Zion, and located on the north side of Jerusalem. In the city, Mount Zion had become a shelter to the city from fierce winds blowing from that quarter. Enemies assembled together against Jerusalem. However, God made their enemies to fear them instead. The Presence of the Lord kept their enemies in check, they came, they saw, and they retreated. It was not Jerusalem that filled the enemy with fear, but the presence and power of the Lord of Hosts. They heard that God was in that city, and that the city had the divine protection of the Almighty God. The enemies were formidable, but unequal to the Omnipotent God.

It is said that "fear took hold upon them and pain as a woman in travail." Labor pains came on them suddenly, and fear compared to the "east wind" that has power to break in pieces a vessel. For who can stand before an angry God? This is an encouraging vision of the church, which God founded upon the rock. As we have heard the promises of God, so we have seen in their fulfillment a vision of stability and the perpetualness of the church. God promises to establish the church forever. For God has said that the gates of hell would not prevail against it. It is a cause to "Selah," to pause and ponder about the faithfulness and greatness of God. God is watching over His church, protecting and preserving it. We have heard that He is Omnipotent, and now we have seen it. We have heard that He cares and now we have seen it. These are God's promises to the church. This was a message of comfort to the church, of the abiding presence of God. Let Mount Zion rejoice. We are encouraged to observe the beauty, strength, providential care bestowed by God, the Divine Caretaker, upon His church. Once we observe that, we are commissioned to communicate that to the next generation. The Psalmists encourages us to "Walk about Zion," and gaze upon the glory and greatness of Our God.

He challenges us to take an all-around view. So at whatever direction you view Mount Zion, you will view the greatness and goodness of our God. Nehemiah walked around the walls, singing and giving praise to God. Nehemiah 12:31, 38-40 says: "Then I brought up the princes of Judah upon the wall, and appointed two great *companies of them that gave* thanks, *whereof one* went on the right hand upon the wall toward the dung gate; The second choir proceeded to the left, while I followed them with half of the people on the wall, above the Tower of Furnaces, to the Broad Wall, and above the Gate of Ephraim, by the Old Gate, by the Fish Gate, the Tower of Hananel and the Tower of the Hundred, as far as the Sheep Gate; and they stopped at the Gate of the Guard. Then the two choirs took their stand in the house of God. So did I and half of the officials with me" (KJV)

We are told to tell the towers, and to mark well the bulwarks. Gaze upon it with wonder, and observe the fullness of their beauty and strength. Pass on what you have observed to the next generation, with this understanding. Despite how formidable their enemies, the towers and bulwarks remained in strength. This was due to the Presence of the Lord of Hosts. It is with this knowledge of His word, that likewise, we are to fortify ourselves. The enemies seek to undo us, but Our God is for us. Take note that the strength of the towers and bulwarks was not physical, as imposing a structure they might have been. This is to be viewed through a spiritual lens. The towers and bulwarks are symbolic representations of objects of faith. The strength in the tower and bulwark was the "Presence of "El- Gibhor, Mighty God" (Isaiah 9:6) and "Eyaluth, Strength" (Psalm 22:19). Likewise, the source of the churches' strength is the Presence of the Almighty God. Jesus said in Matthew:

"And I tell you that you are Peter, and on this rock I will build my church, and the gates of Hades will not overcome it" (Matthew 16:18 NIV). The church is fortified and strengthened by the power and presence of God. This is a Psalm of triumph in God and His faithfulness. It is the blessed assurance that He will protect, provide, and establish the church that He founded upon the Rock. This is the story that we, His people, must pass on to posterity. God, Almighty, the Uncreated One, the Unmoved Mover assures us in His word that He who remains Omnipotent, Omniscient, Immutable, and Eternal will guide us with His eye.

*"For there shall be a day, that the watchmen upon the mount Ephraim shall cry, Arise ye, and let us go up to Zion unto the LORD our God"* (Jeremiah 31:6 KJV).

The refrain of the old gospel hymn goes:

*We're marching to Zion, Beautiful, beautiful Zion; We're marching upward to Zion, The beautiful city of God.*[32]

"But you have come to Mount Zion, the city of the living God, the heavenly Jerusalem, and to myriads of angels, to the assembly [23]and congregation of the firstborn, who are enrolled in heaven, and to God, the judge of all, and to the spirits of the righteous, who have been made perfect,[24] and to Jesus, the mediator of a new covenant, and to the sprinkled blood that speaks of something better than Abel's does" (Hebrews 12:22-24 NET).

We have come to Mount Zion with joy, not Mount Sinai with fear and trepidation. This is a heavenly place, the city of the living God. We have joined by faith a heavenly company, a universal

---

[32] Isaac Watts, *We're marching to Zion,* (1707).

church. God who judges all, and Jesus the mediator of a new covenant. Jesus's blood, which speaks for us of better things than Abel. His blood speaks to His father on our behalf. His blood speaks to the lost, on God's behalf. We are encouraged to march onward to Zion.

The passage in Micah 4:1-2 states the following: "But in the latter days, it will happen that the mountain of the house of the Lord will be established on the top of the mountains, and it will be exalted above the hills; and peoples will stream to it. And many nations shall come and say, "Come, and let us go up to the mountain of the Lord, and to the house of the God of Jacob; and he will teach us of his ways, and we will walk in his paths; for the law shall go forth of Zion and the word of the Lord from Jerusalem. " (KJV)

# The Mountain of the Lord

*"In the future the LORD's Temple Mount will be the most important mountain of all; it will be more prominent than other hills. People will stream to it. Many nations will come, saying, "Come on! Let's go up to the LORD's mountain, to the temple of Jacob's God, so he can teach us his commands and we can live by his laws." For Zion will be the source of instruction; the LORD's teachings will proceed from Jerusalem"* (Micah 4:1-2 NET)

*"For there shall be a day, that the watchmen upon the mount Ephraim shall cry, Arise ye, and let us go up to Zion unto the LORD our God"* (Jeremiah 31:6 KJV)

*"And it shall come to pass that whoever calls on the name of the Lord Shall be saved. For on Mount Zion and in Jerusalem, there shall be deliverance, As the Lord has said among the remnant that the Lord calls "* (Joel 2:32b CLB)

## Location, Location, Location

*"After this I looked, and, behold, a door was opened in heaven: and the first voice which I heard was as it were of a trumpet talking with me; which said, Come up hither, and I will shew thee things which must be hereafter"*
(Revelations 4:1 KJV)

*"But a time is coming - and now is here - when the true worshipers will worship the Father in spirit and truth, for the Father seeks such people to be his worshipers. God is spirit, and the people who worship him must worship in spirit and truth"*
(John 4:23-24 NET)

*"He had a dream, and behold, a ladder was set on the earth with its top reaching to heaven; and behold the angels of God were ascending and descending on it. And behold, the Lord stood above it and said. "I Am the Lord, the God of your father Abraham and the God of Isaac"* (Genesis 28:12-13 Amp).

In Ezekiel 1:1 we read this, "Now it came to pass in the thirtieth year, in the fourth month, on the fifth day of the month, as I was among the captives by the River Chebar, that the heavens were opened and I saw visions of God" (KJV). The name Ezekiel means God is strong, or God strengthens. Note that the location of Ezekiel was near the "river," symbolizing the "Holy Spirit and a place of prayer." It is there where Ezekiel received the vision. In Revelations, Chapter one, John says "I was in the spirit on the Lord's day and I heard behind me a loud voice, as if a trumpet, saying "I Am the Alpha and Omega, the First and the Last," and "What you see write in a book and send it to the seven churches…" (Revelations 1:10-11 CLB)

**Revelations come in the presence of the Lord**

The church is being called into a deeper relationship and revelation of Our Heavenly Father's love. The God of Abraham, Isaac, and Jacob is calling us through His Son to walk in such a manner that we are invited to "Come up here" and hear what the spirit is saying to the church, now. The body of Christ needs a corporate "Issachar anointing" to understand the times and the seasons, and know what to do for the people. We are being called into deeper levels of spiritual intimacy, worship, and then service. The vision for the future comes when we dwell in the secret place of the Most High God. John in the Book of Revelations, chapter 5, describes how worship spread from the center near the throne, outwardly. It expands from the angels, to the creatures, and to the elders.

"Then I looked, and I heard the voice of many angels around the throne, numbering thousands upon thousands, and ten thousand times ten thousand. They encircled the throne and the living creatures and the elders. In a loud voice they sang: "Worthy is the

Lamb, who was slain to receive power and wealth and wisdom and strength and honor and glory and praise!" Then I heard every creature in heaven and on earth and under the earth and on the sea and all that is in them, singing "To Him who sits on the throne and to the Lamb be praise and honor and glory and power for ever and ever! The four living creatures said, Amen, "and the elders fell down and worshipped" (Revelations 5:11-14 NIV)

In his booklet "Surviving the Last Days," Derek Prince wrote, "The worship spread outward from the throne, to the angels, then to every creature in the universe. And they are all united in praising God. So follow the outline of what God presents here: His concern for the churches is first and foremost, and the throne room of God is filled with the expanding throngs of those in worship"[33] He concludes that if you face the future without God's vision or perspective, it may prove difficult to endure.

The only thing that can sustain us in times of adversity is the true love for God. It is time for us to purify ourselves from everything that contaminates our body and soul, perfecting holiness out of reverence for God. In Hosea we are encouraged "Come, let us return to the Lord. For He has torn us, but He will bandage us. He will revive us after two days; He will raise us up on the third day. That we may live before Him. So let us know, let us press on to know the LORD. His going forth is as certain as the dawn; And He will come to us like the rain. Like the spring rain

---

[33] Derek Prince, *Surviving the Last Days, #4382 How to Face the Last Days Without Fears*, 2004, p. 29.

watering the earth" (Hosea 6:1-3 NAS). A real estate agent will tell you "Location is everything." John was in the right location to hear what the Spirit of God had to say to the church. It's time to climb Jacob's ladder, climbing up from earth to heaven, each round goes higher and higher. May we arise as soldiers of the cross.

## Come Up Here

formerly, "There's a Great Camp Meeting")[34]

Walk together, children
Don't you, don't you get weary
There's a great camp meeting
And it's in the promised land

Sing together children
Don't you, don't you get weary
There's a great camp meeting and it's in the promised land
Sing to him a new song
Sing in harmony
Heaven sent melodies
Sound so sweet to me
Just sounds sweet to me

---

[34] John W. Work from "American Negro Songs" 1940 and adapted by Jan Granger ©2013 based upon the song formerly written as "There's a Great Camp Meeting"

Dance together, children

Don't you , don't get weary

There's a great camp meeting

And it's in the promised land

Praise Him with dancing feet

Hear heavenly frequencies

Pick up the Spirit's rhythm and beat

Dance in the Spirit

The life of God is in it

Get your groove on, groove on, yeah


Pray together children

Don't you, don't'' get weary

There's a great camp meeting in the

Pray on one accord

Build the walls and hold on to the Spirit's sword

Won't be long till you get your reward

There's a great camp meeting and it's in the promised land


I have mourned, but I will not tire

I have mourned, but I will not tire

I have mourned, but I will not tire

There's a great camp meeting in the promised land


Come up here,

Breathe in glory's atmosphere

See heavens lights

Hear joyful sounds

Take off your shoes

It's holy ground


Come on up and walk with me come on up

And sing a new song

Come on up here and

Do a little dance

Come on up and

Pray with me

Come on up

And shout victory


Walk with me

Sing a new song

Do a little dance

Pray with me

Shout victory

Come on up here

Come on up here


Come on up here

Heavenly places

New Atmospheres

New Atmospheres

Come on, come on up here

Come on, come on up here

# So Great a Cloud of Witnesses

*"Therefore since such a great cloud of witnesses surrounds us, let us throw off everything that hinders and the sin that so easily entangles, and let us run with perseverance the race marked out for us. Let us fix our eyes on Jesus, the Author and Perfector of our faith, who for the joy set before Him endured the cross, scorning its shame, and sat down at the right hand of the throne of God"*
(Hebrews12: 1-2 NIV).

The devil cannot erase what God has purposed. Sooner or later God connects His body with history to establish what He has determined. What began on Azusa Street and in other places that have seen the glory of God will again be relieved by His Body in this age.[35] It is clear from this passage that we are in a race begun by those who have gone on before us. In Hebrews, chapter11 we find a record of the Bible's greatest heroes of faith.

The "greatest heroes of faith" and "so great a cloud of witnesses" are linked in this passage by the word "also." Those heroes of faith make up the cloud of witnesses that are possibly

---

[35] Ana Mendez Ferrell, Eat My Flesh, Drink My Blood, Voice of the Light; 2 edition (August 1, 2008), p. 110.

looking down on us right now. I can't help but wonder what they see.

There are others who serve to inspire us and encourage us on, by example, as we run our leg of the race. I'd like to pay tribute to other heroes of faith, maybe unknown to most. In Thomas C. Oden's book, How Africa Shaped The Christian Mind, it states the following, "For African believers the martyrs pointed to the continuity of the communion of the saints. They bore their cross in Africa."[36] In Oden's book, is the following in the chapter "How the Blood of African Martyrs Became the Seed of European Christianity:" Early African Believers gave a lasting gift to world Christianity. The gift was not given without blood or torture. Africa suffered wider and heavier persecutions, tortures, beheadings, and martyrdoms than elsewhere.[37]

There is a riveting account of two young North African women, Perpetua and Felitcitus, who were killed, along with some companions, on March 7,203 at Carthage. It is particularly gripping because Feliicitas, Perpetua's household slave, was pregnant at the time they were apprehended and Perpetua was nursing her young child. They were thrown into an arena where they were tossed and crushed by animals:

> "For the young women, however, the Devil had
> prepared a mad heifer. This was an unusual

---

[36] Thomas C. Oden, How Africa Shaped The Christian Mind, (IVP Academic, 2010), p. 117.
[37] Ibid. p. 124.

animal, but it was chosen that their sex might be matched with that of the beast. So they were stripped naked, placed in nets and thus brought out into the arena. Even the crowd was horrified when they saw that one was a delicate young girl and the other was a woman fresh from childbirth with the milk still dripping from her breasts. And so they were brought back again and dressed in unbelted tunics. Ah, most valiant and blessed martyrs! Truly are you called and chosen for the glory of Christ Jesus our Lord! And any man who exalts, honors, and worships his glory should read for the consolation of the Church these new deeds of heroism which are no less significant than the tales of old. For these new manifestations of virtue will bear witness to one and the same Spirit who still operates, and to God the Father Almighty, to his Son Jesus Christ our Lord, to who is splendor and immeasurable power for all the ages. Amen."[38]

Simon of Cyrene, the father of Alexander and Rufus upon whom the cross-had been laid, was of African descent from Cyrene. The people of Cyrene were African people. Cyrene, now known as Libya, located along the Mediterranean coast of North

---

[38] From The Acts of the Christian Martyrs Texts and translation by Herbert Musurillo, (Oxford University Press, 1972), p. 10-11.

Africa. It is important to note that in Biblical times there were not Arab people but Africans living there. Simon was in Jerusalem during the Passover celebration. Out of the entire crowd he was compelled to bear the cross by the Roman soldiers in the final mile of Jesus's earthly journey. "As they led him away, they seized Simon of Cyrene, who was coming in from the country. They placed the cross on his back and made him carry it behind Jesus" (Luke 23:26 NET). Was this juncture a defining moment, or merely a chance encounter with the Son of God? Can there be a chance encounter with the Son of God? The destiny of Jesus, the Son of God, and a man of African descent cross at a pivotal time in history. Wow! There are men of God who have suggested that this may be a metaphorical representation of what God may require of people of African descent. Simon rose to the occasion and carried the cross with Jesus. We are indeed surrounded by so great a cloud of witnesses.

Another group of "Heroes I want to pay tribute to are the black Christian Abolitionists considered by many as forgotten. They were not just "forerunners for racial justice and equality," but viewed slavery as a sin. Though despised and loathed by others, they bore the cause of the "enslaved" for a span of thirty years. These men and women carried a cross and fought the good fight of faith. Heroes and Heroines like Sojourner Truth.[39] Her birth name was Isabella Baumfree. She was born in slavery, but managed to escape with her daughter to freedom in 1826. Then Sojourner

---

[39] Sojourner Truth (1797- November 26, 1883).

Truth aided in the recruitment of black soldiers for the Union army.

Harriet Tubman's[40] birth name was Araminta Harriet Ross. She was born a slave. Harriet became known as the "Moses of her people," as she helped in excess of 300 slaves escape by way of the underground railroad and safe houses. She eventually returned to Dorchester County Md., bringing slaves north.

Fredrick Douglas,[41] was known as statesman, reformer, and writer/orator. He escaped slavery and rose to a position of leadership in the abolitionist movement. His oratorical skills proved that slaves indeed possessed intellectual capacities.

William Still,[42] was born in Burlington County, New Jersey and became a member of the abolitionist movement and an Underground Railroad conductor. He was known as a businessman, activist, and writer. Still wrote a book on the Underground Railroad, and he kept records for slave's relatives. The first Black YMCA was founded with Still's help.

Olaudah Eqoiano[43] (1745-1797) is also known by his slave name, Gustavus Vassa. Equiano wrote his autobiography, *The Interesting Narrative of the Life of Olaudah Equiano*. In this narrative he describes the atrocities of slavery, which aided the British lawmakers in the demise of slavery.

---

[40] Harriet Tubman's (1820- March 10,1913).
[41] Fredrick Douglas (February 1818-February 20, 1895).
[42] William Still (October 7,1821-July 14,1902).
[43] Olaudah Eqoiano (1745-1797).

I also pay tribute to others like William Joseph Seymour, the Azusa Street Mission founder. He was the leader of the Pentecostal revival, which gave birth to a movement in 1906. It was considered one of the greatest revivals since Pentecost, called the Great Azusa Street Awakening, which traveled from Los Angeles, California to Chicago Illinois. There were conversions to Christ, manifestations of healings, and deliverances from demonic bondages. William Seymour predicted that in 100 years there would be another great awakening that would exceed their experience.

Mother Elizabeth J. Dabney,[44] a notable African-American woman of prayer, wrote an article entitled "What It Means To Pray Through," which gave birth to a worldwide prayer movement. She and her husband Elder E.H. Dabney began a work in a mission in Philadelphia. The neighborhood was undeniably "wrought with violence and danger." But she vowed to God that she would pray day and night for the span of three years, meeting God in a certain location, seeking his face and favor. She also vowed to fast for 72 hours for two years. She said that she kneeled on the floor to pray until the "skin wore off her knees. While fasting, she stayed at the church, refusing to go home and sleep. It is at that juncture that she entered into prayer ministry. Soon Mother Dabney's testimony was featured in the Pentecostal Evangel. God answered her prayers and the mission grew. In access of three million letters flowed in worldwide inquiring about "praying through."

---

[44] Mother Elizabeth J. Dabney, (1925).

I echo the words in Hebrews; so great a cloud of witnesses surrounds us. May we rise to the occasion.

# Let Justice Roll Down Like a River

*"But let justice run down as waters, and righteousness as a mighty stream"* (Amos 5:24 KJV).

*"And what does the Lord require of you? To act justly, and to love mercy and to walk humbly with your God"* (Micah 6:8 NIV).

*"I know that the LORD defends the cause of the oppressed and vindicates the poor"* (Psalm140:12 NET).

*"A father of the fatherless, and a defender of the widows, is God in his holy habitation"* (Psalm 68:5 WEB).

The character of God is revealed in His word. He is reveals himself as a father of the fatherless and defender of widows. In Psalm 89:14, It states that righteousness and justice are the foundation of God's throne. Psalm 103:6 states "The Lord executes righteousness and justice for all the oppressed." African–Americans are among the groups that have suffered under a yoke of oppression. In Psalm140:12 God promises that He will maintain the cause of the afflicted, and justice for the poor. I asked a question in a previous chapter—where do we go for redress. To whom shall we go as a people to seek justice? In Derek Prince's book, *Orphans, Widows, The Poor and Oppressed*,[45] he describes the requirements for righteousness. Job says that he put on righteousness and it clothed him. He said, "My justice was like a robe and a [diadem] or turban" (Job 29-14 NIV). The Bible also says:"All have sinned and come short of the glory of God" (Romans 3:23 KJV). Job understood we have no righteousness of our own. He goes on to state what righteousness looks like when he says, "I was eyes to the blind, and I was feet to the lame. I was a father to the poor, and I searched out the case that I did not know. I broke the fangs of the wicked and plucked the victim from his teeth" (Job 29:15-17 NIV). The Prophet Isaiah says, "Wash yourselves, make yourselves clean; Put away the evil of your doings from before my eyes. Cease to do evil; Learn to do good; Seek justice, Rebuke the oppressor; Defend the fatherless; Plead for the widow" (Isaiah 1:16-17 NIV). Isaiah continues by tying these words about God to His Son, Jesus, "Concerning Jesus, the Messiah it is prophesied there shall come forth a rod from the stem of Jesse, and a branch shall grow out of His roots. The Spirit of the Lord shall rest upon Him. The Spirit of wisdom and understanding, the Spirit of counsel and might, The Spirit of knowledge and of the fear of the Lord. His delight is in the fear of the Lord, and He shall not judge by the sight of His eyes, but with righteousness He shall judge the poor, and decide with equity for the meek of the earth

---

[45] Derek Prince, Orphans, *Who Cares for Orphans, Widows, the Poor and Oppressed, God Does...Do We?* (Derek Prince Ministries-UK (February 2000).

(Isaiah 11:1-4a NIV). Scripture clearly reveals God's concern for the plight of the poor.

As priest God has given us authority to rule. In Romans 5:17 it states that "For if by one man's offence death reigned by one; much more they which receive abundance of grace and of the gift of righteousness shall reign in life by one, Jesus Christ" (KJV).

Death reigned as a consequence of Adam's sin, but Christ's righteousness secured our freedom and positioned us to reign in this present life. So salvation is a restorative process to a position of authority and dominion. In 1 Peter 2:5 those in Christ are identified as a holy priesthood. As priest we are to offer to God spiritual sacrifices, such as prayer, thanksgiving, worship. As Walter Wink, in his article "History Belongs to the Intercessors"[46] says, we are the designated ones to change the course of history. There are various examples of "Prophets" in the Bible whose prophetic words altered the course of history. One example is Jeremiah, who at a young age was appointed by God and placed over nations and kingdoms. The messages of prophets have often been meet with disdain. Such was the case with Jeremiah. However, careful examination of the Bible bears out that his words spoken under the unction of the Holy Spirit prevailed. Derek Prince is his book, Shaping History through Prayer and Fasting,[47] put it succinctly, "In all earths affairs the last word is with God."

---

[46] Walter Wink, "History Belongs to the Intercessors" from Understanding Spiritual Warfare: Four Views (Baker Academic (December 1, 2012).
[47] Derek Prince, Shaping History through Prayer and Fasting (Whitaker House (June 1, 2002).

Psalms 103:19 states, "The LORD has established his throne in heaven; his kingdom extends over everything" (NET). First Timothy 2:1-4 gives us a look at where some of prayers need to be directed, "Therefore I exhort first of all that supplications, prayers, intercessions, and giving of thanks be made for all men, for kings and all who are in authority, that we may live a quiet and peaceable life in all godliness and reverence" (CLB). Thus, we are called to pray for good government, for our President regardless of who that person is, and all those in authority. It is stated in 1 Timothy 2, "For this is good and acceptable in the sight of God our Savior" As watchman and watchwomen, we are instructed to pray. Derek Prince presents these simple steps from 1 Timothy 2:1-4: 1.The first ministry and outreach of believers meeting together in regular fellowship is prayer. 2. The first topic for prayer is good government. 3. We are to pray for good government. 4. God desires all men to have the truth of the gospel preached to them. 5. Good government facilitates the preaching of the gospel, while bad government hinders it. Therefore good government is the will of God."[48]

We as watchmen/ intercessors are obliged to extend our prayers beyond ourselves and be watchful for our churches, government, the nations, the poor, oppressed and disenfranchised. As a kingdom and as priests we are in a position to seek God's divine intervention and ask for justice according to His word. Those prayers can alter the course of history. We need to pray for

[48] Ibid. p. 42.

the church, that at this time in history, we will arise and shine. We are also instructed in His word to pray for Jerusalem. In Psalm 122:6, it admonishes us to pray for the peace of Jerusalem. Then it offers these words of promise if we pray: May those who love you be secure. May there be peace within your walls and security within your citadels.

The scriptures in the Bible concerning justice are vast. We can apply the authority of Gods written word over any situation, given we meet the requirements. I would like to suggest some specific scriptures, obviously not exhaustive that we can pray when dealing with various issues related to strongholds of injustice. In Isaiah 49:2, it is stated that "He made my mouth like a sharpened sword, in the shadow of His hand He hid me; He made me into a polished arrow" (NIV). When God's Word is proclaimed or prayed in the power of the Holy Spirit, it transforms into "the sword of the Spirit." In Hebrews 4:12, it states, "For the word of God is living and active. Sharper than a double edged sword, it penetrates even to dividing soul and spirit, joints and marrow; it judges the thoughts and the attitudes of the heart" (NIV) It is with this sword that the strongholds will come crashing down in your life, in the lives of those you love, and in the lives of the People of God. When the child of God offers these types of prayers with humility, they are heard. Jesus set the example in Hebrews 5:7: "During the days of Jesus's life on earth, He offered up prayers and petitions with loud cries and tears to the One who could save Him from death, and He was heard…" (NIV). God declares in Jeremiah

51:20: "You are My war club; My weapon for battle, with you I will shatter nations, with you I will destroy kingdoms, with you I will destroy horse and rider, with you I will shatter man and woman, with you I will shatter old man and youth, with you I will shatter young man and maiden, with you I will shatter Shepard and flock, with you I will shatter farmer and oxen, with you I shatter governor and officials" (NIV). As we avail ourselves to God, He uses us as instruments for the destruction of yokes of oppression.

In the late 1970's I persistently interceded concerning the issue of apartheid in South Africa. During the years between 1978 and 1989 P.W. Botha served as prime minister and President of the South African government. He enforced the racial segregation through the system of apartheid. Out of concern for those suffering under such a strict system, I began praying a modified version Psalm 75:10. Derek Prince had used the scripture in a similar fashion, described in his book. Inspired by his account, I prayed, "Lord raise up the righteous and put down the wicked in South Africa." I felt very comfortable with that prayer, because it's left up to God to determine those who are righteous and those who are wicked. In February 1989 F.W. De Klerk succeeded P.W Botha as National Party Leader and worked with Nelson Mandela to bring that cruel system to an end. With that began the dismantling of the rigid, unjust system of apartheid. I thanked God for His faithfulness in moving on behalf of the oppressed. "Not by power, not by might, but by My Spirit, says the Lord Almighty" Zechariah

(4:6). It is my prayer that Justice rolls down into (America) and His righteousness like a never failing stream. Will you join me?

## Arrows of Deliverance

*"So the poor have hope and injustice shuts its mouth."*

*Job 5:16 NIV*

**Jeremiah 21:12b NET**
The LORD says: 'See to it that people each day are judged fairly. Deliver those who have been robbed from those who oppress them. Otherwise, my wrath will blaze out against you. It will burn like a fire that cannot be put out because of the evil that you have done.

**Jeremiah 23:29 NET**
My message is like a fire that purges dross! It is like a hammer that breaks a rock in pieces! I, the LORD, so affirm it!

**Deuteronomy 16:19 WEB**
You shall not wrest justice: you shall not respect persons; neither shall you take a bribe; for a bribe does blind the eyes of the wise, and pervert the words of the righteous.

**Psalm 72:12-13b WEB**
For he will deliver the needy when he cries; the poor, who has no helper.

**Psalm 72:1,4 KJV**
Give the king thy judgments, O God, and thy righteousness unto the king's son.
He shall judge the poor of the people, he shall save the children of the needy, and shall break in pieces the oppressor.

**Psalm 7:9-10 WEB**
Oh let the wickedness of the wicked come to an end, but establish the righteous; their minds and hearts are searched by the righteous God. My shield is with God, who saves the upright in heart.

**Psalm 82:3-4 KJV**
Defend the poor and fatherless: do justice to the afflicted and needy. Deliver the poor and needy: rid *them* out of the hand of the wicked.

**Psalm 142:6-7** NIV
Listen to my cry, for I am in desperate need; rescue me from those who pursue me, for they are too strong for me. Set me free from my prison that I may praise your name. Then the righteous will gather about me because of your goodness to me.

**Psalm 146:6 NET**
the one who made heaven and earth, the sea, and all that is in them, who remains forever faithful, vindicates the oppressed, and gives food to the hungry. The Lord releases the imprisoned.

**Psalm 133: 1-3 KJV**
Behold, how good and how pleasant *it is* for brethren to dwell together in unity! *It is* like the precious ointment upon the head, that ran down upon the beard, *even* Aaron's beard: that went down to the skirts of his garments; As the dew of Hermon, *and as the dew* that descended upon the mountains of Zion: for there the LORD commanded the blessing, *even* life for evermore.

**Isaiah 25:4** WEB
For you have been a stronghold to the poor, a stronghold to the needy in his distress, a refuge from the storm, a shade from the heat, when the blast of the dreaded ones is like a storm against the wall.

**Ezekiel 34:27b** NET
They will know that I am the LORD, when I break the bars of their yoke and rescue them from the hand of those who enslaved them.

**Psalm 89:14 NET**
Equity and justice are the foundation of your throne. Loyal love and faithfulness characterize your rule.

**Isaiah 11:3 WEB**
His delight will be in the fear of Yahweh. He will not judge by the sight of his eyes, neither decide by the hearing of his ears;

**Psalm 70 NET**
O God, please be willing to rescue me!
O Lord, hurry and help me!
May those who are trying to take my life
be embarrassed and ashamed!
May those who want to harm me
be turned back and ashamed!
May those who say, "Aha! Aha!"
be driven back and disgraced!
May all those who seek you be happy and rejoice in you!
May those who love to experience your deliverance say continually,
"May God be praised!"
I am oppressed and needy!
O God, hurry to me!
You are my helper and my deliverer!
O Lord, do not delay!

**Psalm 35:10** NET
With all my strength I will say,
"O Lord, who can compare to you?
You rescue the oppressed from those who try to overpower them;
the oppressed and needy from those who try to rob them."

**Psalms 44:4-8 NET**
You are my king, O God!
Decree Jacob's deliverance!
By your power we will drive back our enemies;
by your strength we will trample down our foes!
For I do not trust in my bow,
and I do not prevail by my sword.
For you deliver us from our enemies;
you humiliate those who hate us.
In God I boast all day long,
and we will continually give thanks to your name. (Selah)

**Deuteronomy 4:37b NET**
Moreover, because he loved your ancestors, he chose their descendants who followed them and personally brought you out of Egypt with his great power

**Psalm 25:15 KJV**
Mine eyes are ever toward the LORD; for he shall pluck my feet out of the net.

**Matthew 12:18 KJV**
Behold my servant, whom I have chosen; my beloved, in whom my soul is well pleased: I will put my spirit upon him, and he shall shew judgment to the Gentiles.

**Isaiah 61:1-4 WEB**
The Lord Yahweh's Spirit is on me;
because Yahweh has anointed me to preach good news to the humble.
He has sent me to bind up the broken hearted,
to proclaim liberty to the captives,
and release to those who are bound;
to proclaim the year of Yahweh's favor,
and the day of vengeance of our God;
to comfort all who mourn;
to provide for those who mourn in Zion,
to give to them a garland for ashes,
the oil of joy for mourning,
the garment of praise for the spirit of heaviness;
that they may be called trees of righteousness,
the planting of Yahweh,
that he may be glorified.
They will rebuild the old ruins.
They will raise up the places long devastated.
They will repair the ruined cities,
that have been devastated for many generations.

**Isaiah 42:1-3 WEB**

"Behold, my servant, whom I uphold;
my chosen, in whom my soul delights—
I have put my Spirit on him.
He will bring justice to the nations.
He will not shout,
nor raise his voice,
nor cause it to be heard in the street.
He won't break a bruised reed.
He won't quench a dimly burning wick.
He will faithfully bring justice.

**Psalm 30:5 KJV**

For his anger *endureth but* a moment; in his favour *is* life: weeping may endure for a night, but joy *cometh* in the morning.

**Isaiah 43:5-7 WEB**

Don't be afraid; for I am with you. I will bring your seed from the east, and gather you from the west. I will tell the north, 'Give them up!' and tell the south, 'Don't hold them back! Bring my sons from far, and my daughters from the ends of the earth—everyone who is called by my name, and whom I have created for my glory, whom I have formed, yes, whom I have made.'"

**Isaiah 49:16-18 WEB**

Behold, I have engraved you on the palms of my hands. Your walls are continually before me. Your children hurry. Your destroyers and those who devastated you will leave you. Lift up your eyes all around, and see: all these gather themselves together, and come to you. As I live," says Yahweh, "you shall surely clothe yourself with them all as with an ornament, and dress yourself with them, like a bride.

**Isaiah 14:3-7 WEB**

It will happen in the day that Yahweh will give you rest from your sorrow, from your trouble, and from the hard service in which you were made to serve, [4]that you will take up this parable against the king of Babylon, and say, "How the oppressor has ceased! The golden city has ceased!"[5]Yahweh has broken the staff of the wicked, the scepter of the rulers, <sup>6</sup>who struck the peoples in wrath with a continual stroke, who ruled the nations in anger, with a persecution that no one restrained. <sup>7</sup>The whole earth is at rest, and is quiet. They break out song.

## Isaiah 45:1-3 WEB
Yahweh says to his anointed, to Cyrus, whose right hand I have held, to subdue nations before him, and strip kings of their armor; to open the doors before him, and the gates shall not be shut:
"I will go before you,
 and make the rough places smooth.
I will break the doors of brass in pieces,
 and cut apart the bars of iron.
I will give you the treasures of darkness,
 and hidden riches of secret places,
that you may know that it is I, Yahweh, who call you by your name,
 even the God of Israel.

## Exodus 15:1-18 NET
Then Moses and the Israelites sang this song to the LORD. They said,
"I will sing to the LORD, for he has triumphed gloriously,
the horse and its rider he has thrown into the sea.
The LORD is my strength and my song,
and He has become my salvation.
This is my God, and I will praise him,
my father's God, and I will exalt him.
The LORD is a warrior,
The LORD is His name.
The chariots of Pharaoh and his army he has thrown into the sea,
and his chosen officers were drowned in the Red Sea.
The depths have covered them,
they went down to the bottom like a stone.
Your right hand, O LORD, was majestic in power,
your right hand, O LORD, shattered the enemy.
In the abundance of Your majesty you have overthrown
those who rise up against you.
You sent forth your wrath;

it consumed them like stubble.
By the blast of Your nostrils the waters were piled up,
the flowing water stood upright like a heap,
and the deep waters were solidified in the heart of the sea.
The enemy said, 'I will chase, I will overtake,
I will divide the spoil;
my desire will be satisfied on them.
I will draw my sword, my hand will destroy them.'
But you blew with Your breath, and the sea covered them.
They sank like lead in the mighty waters.
Who is like you, O LORD, among the gods?
Who is like You?—majestic in holiness, fearful in praises, working
wonders?
You stretched out Your right hand,
the earth swallowed them.
By Your loyal love you will lead the people whom you have
redeemed;
You will guide them by Your strength to Your holy dwelling place.
The nations will hear and tremble;
anguish will seize the inhabitants of Philistia.
Then the chiefs of Edom will be terrified,
trembling will seize the leaders of Moab,
and the inhabitants of Canaan will shake.
Fear and dread will fall on them;
by the greatness of Your arm they will be as still as stone
until Your people pass by, O LORD,
until the people whom You have bought pass by.
You will bring them in and plant them in the mountain of Your
inheritance,
in the place you made for your residence, O Lord,
the sanctuary, O LORD, that Your hands have established.
The LORD will reign forever and ever!

**Psalm 24:7-8 NET**
Look up, you gates!
Rise up, you eternal doors!
Then the majestic king will enter!
Who is this majestic king?
The LORD who is strong and mighty!
The LORD who is mighty in battle!

**Ezekiel 37:1-6 ESV**
The hand of the Lord was on me, and He brought me out in the Spirit of the Lord and set me down in the middle of a valley; it was full of bones. And He led me around among them, and behold, there were very many on the surface of the valley, and behold, they were very dry. And He said to me, "Son of man, can these bones live?" And I answered, "O Lord God, You know." Then He said to me, "Prophesy over these bones, and say to them, O dry bones, hear the word of the Lord. Thus says the Lord God to these bones: "Behold, I will cause breath to enter you, and you shall live. And I will lay sinews upon you, and will cause flesh to come upon you, and cover you with skin, and put breath in you, and you shall live, and you shall know that I am the Lord."

**Revelation 3:7-8 ESV**
To the church in Philadelphia write:
The words of the holy One, the true One, who has the key of David, who opens and no one will shut, who shuts and no one opens. I know your works. Behold, I have set before you an open door, which no one is able to shut. I know that you have but little power, and yet you have kept My word and have not denied My name."

### Here Comes the Sun

The Beatles

*But unto you who fear My name shall the Sun of Righteousness arise with healing in His wings...(Malachi 4:2, NIV)*